PRACTIC... ...
TO SUCCESS

How to Pursue Your Purpose

BY

DAVE A. SMART

Firstly, I would like to thank God for giving me the wisdom to write this book, my lovely family for all the encouragement and time I spent engrossed in the writing process, my friends and everyone who has added to my lived experiences that have led to the birth of this book. I hope that this book will spark a yearning for the discovery and fulfilment of your purpose.

CONTENTS

INTRODUCTION

Over the past 10 years, I have been searching for answers regarding my purpose in life, I have been trying to answer the most important question in my life, and that is this "what is it that I am here on earth for?." I always knew that I am gifted and that there was a bigger picture for my life, however, I also knew that this process would not be the easiest one, and nor did I take it likely. I was by no means naive into thinking that I would wake up the next day and know definitively what my purpose was/is. In my search to finding out my purpose, I attempted so many avenues and business ventures from selling T-shirts, mobility scooters to making music. I even considered making a career out of playing football and attended semi-professional trials for some top football clubs. Unfortunately, none of these worked in my favour, and I now understand that just because I can do something with ease, doesn't necessarily mean that it is what I should be doing. Instead, I must channel my energy towards what is most important and beneficial for me in the long run.

In 2017 I decided to go back to university to study for my Master of Science in Quantity Surveying, and it was during this period that I signed up for the university's entrepreneur hub known as 'The Hive'. I signed up because I had developed an idea for a sock brand, and I needed assistance with advice to bring the idea to fruition. It was during this period that I was paired with a business councillor, who for purpose of the book will be referred to as Stuart. I met with Stuart for the first time and presented what I thought were amazing designs, and he turned to me instantly and said "I don't think that this idea will work because it requires a lot of capital to get it off the ground – but you should stick around maybe you might come up with another idea with time." As you can imagine I was distraught at the thought that my idea felt like it was being shut down before it had been given a chance to thrive. Fast forward a few weeks later, I had an epiphany and my purpose had been starring me in the face all along. What's interesting about all of this is that people around me had long identified this gift in me, except myself. I kept looking elsewhere because surely my purpose cannot come by so easily in something I do effortlessly day-in-day-out. This is something that I have noticed in others also, where they are extremely gifted, and yet they do not see what's right in front of them. Today I am the founder and director of Inspire Speaking, a limited company that specialises in empowering and equipping people from all walks of life on the art of speaking effectively through our bespoke public speaking masterclasses combined with our skills and experience. Some of our clients include the University of Nottingham, Nottingham City Council, Bluecoat School but to name a few. In addition to running my public speaking company, I am a Quantity Surveyor by profession having worked on various construction projects with values varying between £5-100 million. I have extensive experience in the highways and housing sector. My journey has not been an easy one but certainly one that has been worth it, and continues to be.

This book was birthed out of the numerous conversations and discussions with friends, family, colleagues, and the public at large around the subject of purpose, and often I have heard expressions of frustrations especially at the fact that a lot of the people I have spoken to don't often know what their purpose is. A musician friend of mine Joe once said, "Whilst I know music is my calling, there's no way I'll ever make a living from it." I was taken aback by this comment and began reassuring my friend and advised him to work on his craft and become the best at it. I assured him that doing this will eventually open doors for him. Today he tours all around the country with his band and makes a living from music. I have come to understand that most people are aware of their innate potential and the fact that they have a unique purpose, however, they don't always have the practical advice they need. This book aims to bridge that gap and help as many people as possible to walk towards their purpose as fast as possible. Practical Keys to Success is not another 10 steps to success or a how-to get rich quick book. The author seeks to help the reader to consider a practical and a common-sense approach towards attaining success in various spheres of life.

I wrote this book as an everyday practical guide to help people that are seeking to find out what their purpose is. I understand the many challenges it takes to find out one's purpose and having gone through some of the ordeals inscribed in this book myself. I can help others to navigate the journey a lot better than they would on their own. I recently heard about the sad passing of Chadwick Boseman, the man who brought us 'Black Panther' a film that broke a lot of boundaries for diversity in the movie industry. In his words, he says "Purpose is an essential element of you. It is the reason you are on the planet at this particular time in history. Your very existence is wrapped up in the things you are here to fulfil ... Remember the struggles along the way are only meant to shape you for your purpose," The aim of this book is to spark the thought and imagination that pushes you towards your purpose, to help you to see the thing that may already be at your disposal that you have long ignored in search of everything else.

A study by Carleton University, Canada, and the University of Rochester Medical Centre, US, which was funded by the US National Institute of Mental Health and the National Institute of Aging found that people with purpose tend to live longer. A total of 6000 volunteers aged between 20 to 70 years old took part in the study.

They were scored using a system of how strongly they felt about some of the following;

- Wandering aimlessly through life.
- Living life one day at a time without a thought for the future.
- Sometimes feeling like all there is to be done is done.

Following this study, death records were monitored over 14 years. It was found that people who died had scored lower on purpose in life and lack of positive relationships with others. Whilst having a purpose may not be fully proven to prolong life, it is fair to say that a life lived full of purpose is fulfilled even if it 20 years' worth, and lack of purpose over 100 years is a wasted one for a world that still yearns for your greatness.

Over the past 15 years, I invested heavily in various business ventures including a successful clothing line that operated for 3 years, stock markets, and more. I have worked every job from cleaning schools, kitchen porter, waitering, warehouse packing, and events steward in different UK venues. Throughout this time, I have always considered each job a learning curve and I did not take any for granted.

I am a firm believer in empowering others to fulfil their full potential, overcome challenges and achieve victories I have passed through this in my journey towards self-discovery, I believe that this book will catapult the reader to new ways of thinking and propel you to finding the answers you have been longing for. This is not a one shoe fits all book, but I believe that the principles and ideas shared within will spark the right conversation that will begin to steer the reader into discovering their full potential.

Sometimes your purpose hinges on hearing the right advice from the right person even though you may not like what you are hearing at that very moment. Find out how this became my reality as I searched for my why and purpose in the coming chapters of the book.

I am passionate about this book because I firmly believe that our prime existence hinges on our ability to live out purpose-filled lives that are instrumental in shaping society at large. I know how long it took me to figure out my purpose and all the trials and errors along the way. I am still defining what this means for my life, however, the difference now is that I know which direction I am headed. This book aims to spark a conversation that will drive individuals to think about what purpose means to them. Additionally, how this translates into what they are currently doing or not.

Sharing my struggles and how I overcame them is the first step to building rapport with my readers.

This book will help you to understand what you need to do going forward to achieve your goals, find your purpose, and walk in it. This book will get you out of your comfort zone and challenge your thinking, it will spark the giant that is already in you. You will get an insight into how I have lost thousands of pounds amongst other things and how I have been able to overcome each challenge.

If you could find out how you can be great and live in your purpose by learning from someone else, would you procrastinate or find out? I would like to think your answer is the latter. In that case, what are you waiting for, dig in and elevate your mental capacity and start on this practical journey to discovering your purpose.

The Practical Keys to Success you are about to read have been proven through Dave Smart's journey in discovering his purpose. Each chapter provides new secrets and practical keys that will help you stay in control of your destiny and future. If you follow the practical keys revealed in this book, there is a higher probability that you will enjoy the rest of your life unburdened by the lack of purpose and sense of direction.

> *"It's not enough to have lived. We should be determined to live for something."*
>
> - WINSTON CHURCHILL

Money Principles: Making Smart Decisions About Money

"If you treat every day of your life as a gift, you'll be unwrapping presents your whole life".

For so many years, I focused on accumulating wealth for the wrong reasons. I desired the latest cars, the biggest house, including everything in between. Over-time, my priorities changed, and quality time with family and friends took center stage. I relished the simpler things in life. This outlook on life helped me to appreciate the things that money cannot buy. The most important thing is "keeping the main thing the main thing," as echoed by Stephen Covey. I made a lot of money at varying periods of my life. I remember investing money in the financial stock market back in 2018, a period I managed to generate circa £45k in the space of 2 months. While that was great, I had abysmal money management skills and ended up losing all my winnings, and for the months that followed, I would go on to struggle financially. Perhaps the most challenging time financially, it was as if I did not have access to £45k a few months back. It was at this time that I promised myself that I would be diligent in my finances and be a good steward. It was also at this point that I started to pay close attention to my finances and became more stringent and calculative. I have no regrets about what happened because it became the highest tuition that taught me a huge lesson, albeit in the hardest way.

I came out a wiser, better, and smart person from this ordeal, and now I am in a position where I can influence and encourage others in the same scenario. More so, I can provide others with practical principles and guidance around how to manage finances effectively and avoid some of the pitfalls that I had to endure along the way. I often hear people say that experience is the best teacher, but I don't agree that this should always be the case. People's experiences should help us to make wiser decisions; besides, research can help avoid pitfalls along the way. A wise man/woman will learn from another person's errors and apply that to determine what they will choose. In simple terms, for example, if you know about the dangers of driving while fatigued and you decide to do it anyway, it would be unwise on your part. Common sense says, "I need to avoid driving while tired because of the dangers I can pose to myself and others."

I think most people can agree that having sufficient finances to a point where payday becomes just that, a payday and not a day you anticipate so highly each month because you are drowning in your overdraft. It takes time for wealth to accumulate but it dissipates. within the twinkle of an eye. I have noticed that most people (myself inclusive) feel better when money is sufficient . For example, whenever I have adequate food in the fridge I tend not to get hungry as often as when I don't have much food in the house. Equally, a lack of money produces the same effect, and in my personal life, I have noticed that when I don't have money. I tend to desire things that I wouldn't ordinarily, but when I have enough money these things do not have the same appeal.

Don't get me wrong money is an excellent tool, and it offers great freedom. Everyone aspires for "Freedom," freedom allows us to do the things that we would not ordinarily do. It enables us to spend more time with our family and friends, to travel whenever we want to, and allows us to take care of those dependent upon us. You must draw a line between how you relate to finance, it should never control you, and should never determine who you are. Evaluate your relationship with money frequently; this way, you will position yourself to have a better relationship with your finances. Use your imagination to envision a healthy relationship with money because "Imagination is everything, it's the preview to life's coming attraction." – Albert Einstein

One of the greatest myths of all time is that the accumulation of monetary wealth equals success and happiness. Over the years we have heard of the various unfortunate atrocities that have happened to the rich and famous such as Marilyn Monroe who had fame, beauty, and money, but it was her internal demons that eventually led to her suicide. In addition, the case of world-renowned Swedish DJ Avicii who committed suicide in 2018 after setting dance floors alight in different parts of the world with his infectious sound. These are some of the people that had what most would consider everything one could ask for, yet they were still going through many afflictions within.

I firmly believe that money is just a resource like any other tool that we use in our day-day lives. For this reason, money is only as good as the person using it. With more money comes great responsibility, and as such, just like any other thing in life failure to steward money accordingly and in line with money principles will have you chasing and never finding it. Whether you have much or very little, the most important thing is to be principled. Indeed, the money will always reveal one's character. In my experience with people, I have observed that if you are a flamboyant, proud, ignorant, and loud individual, the accumulation of wealth will only enhance that characteristic in you. By the same token, if you are humble, kind, and thoughtful of others even with the little you have – accumulating more will only accentuate those characteristics within you. After all, it was Napoleon Hill that said "Money is either a good or bad influence, according to the character of the person who possesses it . . . money has no character, no personality, and no values. Its actions reflect the desires of its owner." Urs Willmann, elaborated on this idea when he said, "Because of its seductive power and potential for addiction, money can ruin a person's character if measured inappropriately." I live by the motto that "If you treat every day of your life as a gift, you'll be unwrapping presents your whole life." This is my way of saying life is not black and white and having money does not equate to happiness. You can achieve real wealth when you begin to accept yourself, finding serenity in simple things, having meaningful relationships and friendships. I believe that to reach your full potential; indeed, you must always be willing and open to serving others, striving to be a positive contributor to society. Sometimes the most "Selfish thing you can do in this world is to help someone else . . . because of the gratification, the goodness that comes to you" – Denzel Washington.

Napoleon Hill shared the same ideology when he said that "As you build your wealth, make sure you build your character by setting aside a portion of your income to help others . . . The primary beneficiary of such noble actions is always the one who gives, not the one who receives"

I believe that you are not only here on earth to only become the best version of yourself and make as much money as you can but that we have a broader responsibility to our communities and those around us by being positive contributors to society at large. Integrate yourself into your society. Aim to leave a legacy behind, make an indelible mark that will never fade. An important question for us all, "what will I be remembered for when I'm gone?" or will you vanish quietly into thin air as if you never existed? You need to start thinking of life in this way, I hope that this perspective gives you clarity and points you in the right direction.

Effective Money Management: Pay it forward

Lao Tzu, a great Chinese philosopher, once said that "A journey of a thousand miles beings with a single step," and this is true for a lot of things we do in life. There is a due process of consistency and diligence that needs to be followed and applied to yield the desired results. It is also true for effective money management; some steps and principles need to be developed to steward and manage finances efficiently and successfully.

One of my mentors Azeem once told me about a friend of his who always opts to purchase branded items, whether it is a new washing machine or a new car. So Azeem asked his friend once about why it is that he keeps purchasing expensive and branded items. The friend's response is one that I will always remember regards to money, he responded: "I am not rich yet to buy cheap." The answer to me was profound for two reasons, the first being that Azeem's friend understood a simple principle about money management. That is when you buy cheap, likely; you will soon need to replace that item. A quality product, on the other hand, albeit on the expensive side saves you a lot of money in the long run, its whole life cycle far outweighs buying cheap. It is a simple principle and one that a lot of people can relate to, the cheaper something is, the lesser the quality in a lot of cases.

On my 21st birthday a few years ago, I bought myself a watch to mark the occasion. It was the most expensive watch compared to all my previous ones. The timepiece was silver and encrusted with diamantes all around. I have looked after it so dearly since its purchase, and I am proud to say that years later, it is still in one piece. The lesson here is that if you spend meaningfully on things

11

of value, you are most likely to take better care of them. It is just a fact of life and psychologically works somehow. Cheap doesn't always mean great, and expensive doesn't always mean quality either, so a degree of common sense must be applied as well. Even more important is to ensure that you do not spend beyond your means, only spend what you can afford and save intentionally. Realize that you are in a lane of your own, the only competition is yourself. Strive to be a better version of yourself regardless of what people around you are doing. Sadly, we live in a world where "We buy things we don't need with money we don't have to impress people we don't like." – Edward Norton

Money is a great tool when used effectively; it is for this reason that Francis Bacon said, "Money is a great servant but makes a terrible master."

You can apply the following steps to help you manage your finances;

- **Be honest with how much you earn versus how much you spend** - Avoid spending beyond your means, and always ensure that you stick to your budget – you can get carried away easily once you have money in your bank account, temporary amnesia suddenly takes over and you forget that when drawing up your budget there wasn't enough left over when you thought about buying an extra trouser. Spend out of the money you have after saving and not before that, this way you are on top of your finances and expenditure.

- **Value every single penny and pound you earn, only then will you appreciate money** - My father always taught me to never walk over any money, whether it be a penny, a pound, or better yet a note of any value. I have always kept this principle in how I treat my money, although it has not always been easy. I firmly believe that until you appreciate and respect a penny, you will never fully appreciate the value of a £/pound. A pound is made up of 100 pennies and if 1 penny is missing then you have 99 pence. Simply put, have an appreciation for money, respect it in its purest form, only then will you be able to accumulate more and have a better relationship with money.

- **Have a financial calendar and budget spreadsheet** - This will help you to understand what you have coming in and how much of it is allocated to bills and what you have as a free balance at the end to determine your savings. I highly recommend that you use an active approach to manage your finances effectively, after all, how do you know where you are going if you have no vision of what a good outcome looks like.

- **Have a clear strategy for any outstanding debts** - The keyword here is sacrifice, we all have luxuries that we like to maintain, however, if you are going to dig yourself out of the hole of debt that you've put yourself in then it will take paying the minimum amount. Consider paying double the amount you owe and take a hit for a short period for long-term freedom. Go through your debts with a fine toothcomb and list out high-interest loans and credit card debts. Aim to pay these off first, this will allow you to reduce the total amount you are paying to each respective lender. Where possible consolidate your debts, this can sometimes offer you a better interest rate. Where possible, consider using the help of friends and family, only do this if you are certain you will be able to pay it back because this can lead to breakdown in family relationships. Always remember who was there for you when you needed help, don't spit back in their face.

- **Live a no-frills lifestyle short-term to achieve your long-term goals and financial freedom** - Ryanair the low-cost airline is best known for being one of the most successful no-frills airlines. Their ethos is around providing passengers with a flight from destination A to B, the idea as many will know is that you pay for any extras such as legroom, luggage, and more. Based on this idea I would suggest that you take a similar approach in your finances when shopping, for instance, buy the shops brand as opposed to a well-known brand. This way you will save a lot of money, eventually, you will get your finances to a healthy place, then you can reward yourself.

- **Don't spend what you do not have** - You have heard the phrase patience is a virtue, the same can be said when it comes to looking after your money. It is indeed tempting to live on borrowed money and get whatever you want whenever you want it. There is absolutely nothing wrong with getting what you need but let it not be at the expense of borrowed money, which will accrue additional interest. Practice self-control in this area and you will see your finances take a whole new trajectory. Remember that "Every time you borrow money, you're robbing your future self." – Nathan W. Morris.

- **Be a conscious consumer and make sure that you have a list when going shopping to avoid spending unnecessarily** - One must pay attention to spending patterns and habits, people tend to make impulsive purchases that are not mandatory nor necessary. I have found myself in this predicament a few times where I have been driving home and all of a sudden I would stop and park right outside my local Tesco shop, and while inside I ask myself "What am I even doing here? I do not need anything in particular, but yet I find myself here looking at random products." I am happy to say that I am now conscious of these distractions and can keep them away. Your situation may be different, and it could be that you order take away every night and you can't help yourself. If only you would cook home meals perhaps you may save a lot of money this way. Consider signing up to a bank that traces and groups your shopping spend into categories, this way you can see where you are spending most of your money and can adjust accordingly. I would suggest providers such as Monzo, who offer great budgeting tools to help you limit your spending.

"When money realizes that it is in good hands, it wants to stay and multiply in those hands."

– IDOWU KOYENIKAN

Time Currency: How to Maximise the Indispensable Value of Time

CHAPTER II

"Better three hours too soon than a minute too late."
- William Shakespeare.

I used to have a big problem with timekeeping, a habit that I had developed during my college and university years. I always said to myself, "I have enough time" when I didn't. You see I saw myself as a last-minute person, still thinking that I had enough time to do things, when in fact, that wasn't the case. "You have enough time, David," is what I used to tell myself. "Why would you leave early and spend more time than necessary waiting for that event to start, when you can get there right on time?" All these are some of the excuses I used to tell myself, but when it came down to it, I always ended up being late.

Why am I talking about time? It is one of the most amazing currencies known to mankind. Interestingly, some people continue to take this currency for granted. They fail to realize and respect the fact that every passing second, minute, and hour is irrecoverable. All we have is a recollection of what happened or didn't happen in the time passed. We cannot bring it back for it becomes just a memory never to be relived or experienced again, at least not in this lifetime. The moment you begin to value time, a lot of things will start to make sense. Between 2015 and 2016 I used to commute to work by bus. I lived 10 miles away from work and got an early bus each morning at 7:30 am, it dropped me outside of work at approximately 8:30 am, given there was no traffic. There were days where blankets won the fight over waking up and I would find myself running for the late bus. On days where I missed both the early and late bus, I would book a taxi, which cost me approximately £20 one way. My monthly bus card was £75 but because of my poor timekeeping, my monthly transport expenditure was always unpredictable, some months I would use the taxi at least 2-4 times and this greatly increased my monthly transport expenditure. A bill of £75 a month would sometimes turn into £140-£160. It was all due to a lack of discipline and preparation on my part.

It is crucial to recognize that the lack of preparation doesn't always cost you monetarily only, but it can also cost you professionally. I remember preparing to meet one of my mentors, the great John Dabrowski, a former England professional basketball player. He is a published author of the 'How to Develop World-Class Mental Resilience' and travels all over the world equipping the corporate leaders around the world on the same topic. I was keen to learn some more about what John does and learn from him since I was pursuing a similar field in public speaking. I knew he would have the critical ingredient that I needed to learn. We arranged a meeting for one Saturday afternoon. I remember looking at the clock two hours after we were scheduled to meet and thinking, "oh no, I missed my meeting with John."

You see this lack of preparation put me in jeopardy of potentially losing a priceless and invaluable opportunity with a great speaker and coach. I called John and apologized for missing the meeting with the reasons why and re-arranged to meet him another day. And when that time came again, I had double booked and forgot to prioritize the meeting with John. I had to apologize; on this occasion, again, John was very accommodating and understanding. But could you imagine if he wasn't? I would have lost the opportunity to meet him for a lifetime. Finally, I met up with John over coffee, we had a fantastic meeting, and I gained a lot of insight from our conversation. Since then, I have been learning a great deal from John. John continues to coach and encourage me along the way.

Planning Keys

- Be practical in your approach to planning and preparing.
- Allow yourself ample time to do your activities.
- Better to be early than late.
- If you have a meeting starting at 10 am and you get there at 10 am it's simple – You're late!
- Build a good relationship with time.
- Control time, not the other way around.
- Use calendars, alarms where necessary, write down your appointments.
- If you respect time, people will respect you, at the same time, failure to adhere to time produces the opposite effect.

We can take some lessons on punctuality from some of our neighbours around the world. For instance, in South Korea, it is considered disrespectful to arrive late for a meeting. In Germany you are expected to arrive at least 10 minutes before a meeting is scheduled to start, any later and you are late. On the other hand, there are countries like Nigeria where a 1 o'clock appointment could well end up taking place at 2 o'clock. This may be the norm in countries like Nigeria, or Morocco, where "Moroccan time" can mean anything between that day, and the next. It is essential to recognize that in light of time being this incredible currency that each of us has in equal measure. The wise thing is to use it efficiently with a sense of productivity and purpose. For once you link time to target and productivity, your outlook on time's importance will draw you to want to make the most of it.

The Art of Expediency – The power of acting 'Now' to achieve maximum productivity in your life.

CHAPTER III

"If you want to achieve something, you can't just stare at the steps, you have to step up the stairs."
- Will Smith

Time is of the utmost importance and should be treated with respect. I am sure that at one point you might have come across the phrase "time is precious, or better yet time is money".

'The art of expediency' as I call it is a vital skill that all people should possess, one that will get you very far in life. I learned a lot of valuable lessons and principles from my late mentor and Pastor Jason Steele. One of which was the need to act intentionally and expediently when making decisions and doing tasks. He picked me up from my parents' home in Nottingham one late afternoon and wanted to take me for a drive as he usually would sometimes. We set off on a trip, he began asking me a series of questions as he would typically do. On this occasion, the line of questioning was mostly about my outlook on life, what my long-term goals and plans were. I remember being asked, "So Dave, what do you do for work these days?" I answered, "I'm looking for a job PJ" as I used to call him affectionately. He probed further, "what kind of job are you looking for, and what skills do you have?" I answered, "I'm looking for a job in customer service, and I cut hair also."

As soon as I mentioned that, without hesitation, he quickly parked his car by the side of the road. He picked up his mobile phone and made a call to a guy I now know as Curtis, soon after I heard him say, "Curtis, how are you? Listen I have Dave here - he's looking for a job as a barber can you please give him a trial at your shop?" He managed to arrange an appointment for me to get a trial. I remember as clear as day that soon after he'd concluded his phone call, he looked at me sternly and asked, "Dave, what did I just do?" I replied, "You just rang Curtis to ask if he has a job to offer," In disagreement, he shook his head and said, "No! I didn't waste time, I just made it happen, and that's what you need to do".

This taught me a vital life lesson about maximizing time and ensuring that productivity is at the core of everything I do. I should never make an excuse when I have every opportunity to deal with a matter or task in the present. Failure to do what I can do today only increases my workload for tomorrow. As my workload increases, my chances of productivity have a high probability of being diminished, and I end up playing catch up. Procrastination will always set you back, you will find that what should have taken a few minutes, a few hours, or even a day ends up taking what seems like forever or simply not happening at all. Considering this, it is without a doubt fair to say that acting quickly has a lot of distinct advantages.

I remember watching an interview where Curtis Jackson (50 cent) the rapper spoke of a scenario involving Jamie Foxx, an actor, singer, record producer, and comedian. According to 50 cent he overheard Jamie Foxx talking to his friends about producing a film.

He was tired of going through the hoops of Hollywood where projects often take an insurmountable time before they are approved and finalised. Instead, he wanted them to undertake projects themselves and quickly. In 50 cent's words, Jamie said, "Look at 50 and them, they just are just making moves and not wasting time, let's make moves too." The moral of the story is, don't wait for people's approval before you step out and do what you need to do in the first place. Always remember that "Approval is a lover who will always break your heart." – Sammy Rhodes. Therefore, go out there and grab the bull by the horns, you don't need anyone's permission to be yourself. Will Smith said, "If you want to achieve something, you can't just stare at the steps, you have to step up the stairs."

Often, I hear people utter phrases such as "once I've got my stuff together, I will start, or, once I have my ducks in a row, I will follow my plan." If you need to go back to study, then, do that, it is never too late, whatever you decide to do-do something. The truth is, life requires those who are bold and have a can-do attitude. And those who are willing to step out in faith even when things don't look like they are making sense, I mean don't get me wrong wisdom is needed too. But those who are willing to step out often place themselves in positions of success because any opportunity that arises along the way finds them ready. It is easy to attract and receive opportunities when you are already on the path for which they appear. Have you ever noticed how hard it is to find a job when you haven't got any? Yet how easy it is to get opportunities when you are gainfully employed? The key is to keep walking, keep showing up because soon enough, the opportunity will find you ready. Imagine how many opportunities you have missed because you were never prepared myself included.

Excuses & Missed Opportunities: The enemy of progress

"God will give you a revelation of ideas, but these will come with an expiry date"

Many days, months, or years spent making up excuses lead to missed opportunities. It is imperative to stay alert and take every opportunity to grow, to learn, and take hold of your destiny. 'Carpe diem' is a Latin saying that means "seize the day." It is imperative that you place yourself in an environment of success and are always ready to take the next step towards your greatness. Ultimately, in whatever field or endeavour you find yourself in, the most fulfilling thing to be able to say at the end of the day is Veni, Vidi, Vici – another Latin saying, translated "I came, I saw, I conquered."

Growing up, I had this passion and desire to pursue film writing, I studied earnestly through novels and various self-help books, watched endless tutorial videos on YouTube. I once had an idea to write a dance film based on the South African dance culture; this was back in 2010. The film was set to become the first South African dance film at the time if it went through successfully.

I started writing the film, and over time managed to complete the script, this was back in 2012. I began shopping around for producers to inject the much-needed capital into the project. I spoke to Mfundi Vundla, one of South Africa's leading and successful producers. He is responsible for the long-running soapie Generations the Legacy, formerly known as Generations. I was due to visit South Africa in 2012, so I proposed that we meet up and sent my script over to Morula Pictures. We exchanged messages, over time, and although Mr. Vundla expressed the potential of the script, he felt the structure needed a little bit more work since I was self-taught.

It was at this moment that I became discouraged and stopped pursuing the film idea. I felt that it would take a very long time trying to figure out who and where to go to get this script polished and therefore my morale vanished in an instant. Two years later in 2014, a friend of mine showed me a trailer of a film that encompassed the same idea. Initially, I was very disappointed thinking that I had wasted time and missed an opportunity, in what could have potentially been my breakthrough film. My film idea was no longer a first, and pursuing it would not make sense anymore, although I believe mine was the original idea. If I were to come out now and do a similar film, I would be seen to be copying the film that is already out.

This whole experience made me realize something I believe is very poignant. Which is, God will give you a revelation of ideas, but these will come with an expiry date, and if you delay, someone else will run with the idea. You may end up not doing the very thing you set out to do initially. Stop making excuses and do it; it depends on you. You will learn along the way as you progress through trial and error because the most crucial thing is to START! Kurt Vonnegut said it best, "We have to continually be jumping off cliffs and developing our wings on the way down." There's a process of training that has to take place until birds are fully confident, and it is then that the bird can fly freely. Chris Smith describes the story of an eagle that thought it was a chicken.

A farmer found an eagle's egg in an abandoned nest, he took it and placed it amongst his chicken. When the egg had hatched, the mother hen reared the eagle as if it was her own. The eagle grew amongst chickens and began acting like a chicken in as far as mannerism. Time went by, and the eagle grew, at this stage, it became apparent that there were differences between the eagle and the chicken. Other birds began telling the eagle that it did not belong where it was and that it was capable of more. The eagle, however, had become accustomed to its environment and did not see this as anything wrong. In brief, an owl eventually convinced the eagle to hop on its back, and as the owl soared higher and higher, the eagle became distressingly uncomfortable. It asked the owl to return it to the ground, but the owl continued to rise even higher. The owl flipped over, causing the eagle to fall fast towards the ground. The owl told the eagle to open its wings and viola; it was now flying and soaring over chickens. So, what are you waiting for? Become who you were meant to be whatever your environment and circumstances, you can change the trajectory of your life. Pick up that book that you need to read, go back to training, and do whatever it takes, take your first step towards that goal you so desire for your life.

No matter how much life knocks you down, keep pressing on. Sylvester Stallone said it better when he said, "It's not about how hard you get hit, but how hard you can get hit and still keep moving forward." I believe one should not pray for a weaker load but pray that your shoulders are strong to bear the weight, for it is where pressure is that there are great spoils.

I was browsing the internet one day, and I came across a short video of Jack Ma, the founder of the billion-dollar company Alibaba. He states, "People often underestimate the power of being surrounded by smart people." He further says that "if you are the smartest person in your group, you are on your way to not achieving much." It is imperative to surround yourself with people who are more intelligent than you. Surround yourself with smart people and your life will never be the same again, you cannot be around that kind of environment and remain the same. Steve Jobs, the late Apple CEO once said: "It doesn't make sense to hire smart people and tell them what to do; we hire smart people, so they can tell us what to do." I remember one day in the summer of 2010 as I sat at home on my couch, thinking about where I could find funding for my community interest company at the time. I grabbed my mobile phone and dialled a friend of mine Terrence, I wanted to catch up and find out how he was doing. And it is during this conversation that I asked him what he was up to business-wise, and he told me he was in the process of applying to a tender for his own company. I enquired further about the details of this funding source, and he shared the details with me and told me the deadline was imminent. After ending the call, I headed straight for my laptop to look it up. It took me just under an hour to complete the application form and submit it.

A few weeks later, a letter dropped at my letterbox, and it was correspondence from the funding company. As I opened the letter, I began to clench my teeth, low and behold. The first word I saw was "congratulations" at the top of the message, my tender was successful. I was ecstatic at this good news, I had secured my first funding for the company. The moral of the story is that being around smart people will rub off on you, and you will excel. As you excel those around you will also be motivated, even those who once motivated you.

Excuses, Excuses, and More Excuses: The moment you act you'll be set free

What if I told you that the secret to your success is reliant on your ability to stop making excuses? Excuses like, "where I come from we don't achieve such great things", settling for less because you think "I don't have the money or capital to start that business", or excuses like, "people like me cannot drive a great car or own a home, and can only get insignificant jobs, and nothing more.

Allen Swoope put it this way, "excuses are useless tools that the fools pick," and so I ask you, which one are you. A fool, or an optimist who sees an opportunity when others see gloom, who sees ideas when others are confused, who sees solutions when others see problems? That my friend is what separates the successful and the unsuccessful.

What if I told you that each and everyone has a purpose? A purpose so great you can't even begin to fathom it, you see we are all different, and that's what makes us unique. No one is insignificant and no one should be made to feel less than valuable than another. No one has the right to tell you how to live your life. To fully live out your purpose and attain success, you will have to take risks and do unusual things. Step out of the box, in fact, think like there's no box. Albert Einstein is popularly known for saying that "insanity is doing the same thing over and over expecting a different result."

It goes without saying that if you were to drive past a speed camera set at a limit of 50mph, and you were driving at 60mph, you would likely receive a speeding ticket. So then, you drove at that speed because you happen to be late for work in the morning because of little or no time management. It is evident, some changes need to happen, some of these include waking up early to allow ample time to get ready and head to work. Besides, you may

29

need to implement further reasonable steps such as sleeping a fair amount of time to account for the extra half an hour you need in the morning.

Ultimately, to be successful you need to be daring, be ambitious, be driven, be courageous, Stephen Hunt said: "if you're not living on the edge you're taking up too much space." What he meant was that you must get out of your comfort zone to accomplish any great feats in life. Similarly, I had a conversation with my brother Gift one evening as we sat at a pub and he said to me that, "When an animal is pushed into the corner, that's when it is most dangerous because the only way to go is facing its fears regardless of what stands in its way." Metaphorically, standing on the edge represents a certain level of risk that must be taken in order to function at the highest level of producing results and maximising one's potential. This is the same reason Jeanette Coron said, "Comfort is the enemy of success." You need to have the kind of attitude that says, "Screw it let's do it," Richard Branson is known as 'Mr. Yes' to his staff at the Virgin Group. He has a reputation for eliminating excuses and applying his screw it let's do it attitude to a lot of concepts and ideas. "There are a million reasons why not, but there is just one great reason why you just must be optimistic and change the status quo." - Gary Vaynerchuk

I want you to repeat the following statement to yourself out loud;

> *Excuses are useless tools that the fools pick.*

A single step towards your goal each day is a step taken forward, and a step missed becomes a gap between you and your goals. Take every opportunity to charge forward each day, small steps eventually add up to a thousand steps. I challenge you to start something you've always wanted to pursue, don't become a friend of excuses. The next time you think of an excuse ask yourself, "Do I want to be a fool?"

Lastly remember that "It's not about the cards you're dealt, but how you play the hand." - Randy Pausch. You are the master of your own destiny, you have the ability to channel it in whichever direction you want. Yes, life will throw challenges your way, that's inevitable, the difference is in how you deal with the challenges thrown at you. Ultimately, "It's not how many times you get knocked down that counts, it's how many times you get back up." – George A. Custer. In the same vein Rocky Balboa, a character portrayed by Sylvester Stallone once said "Life's not about how hard of a hit you can give . . . It's about how many you can take, and still keep moving forward." In other words, just because life does not go according to plan, it does not mean you have to give up on your future. Things are always changing, and as the environment around you changes. It's all about you taking control and creating a future that you envisage.

Take charge, use every object that is thrown at you to create a masterpiece of a life. The cliché is that "When life throws you lemons, take them and make lemonade." This couldn't be truer and speaks a lot of our ability to turn every situation around in our favour. Sometimes you don't know just how strong you are until reality demands you to apply that strength. Sometimes you don't know how strong you are until you have no choice but to be strong.' You do not know how patient you are until you have no choice but to wait for those health results, and it seems you have been waiting for eternity. The truth is you have it in you to turn any situation around while you are still alive. Someone somewhere is relying on you to live up to your dreams; considering the reality that you may be the key missing in the achievement of their goals. I think that this realization will get anybody who wants to be somebody off their backs and onto the field. You see, there are a lot of opportunities and yet a few players who are willing to play their part. Don't be the type of person who only wants to see results without working for them, strive to be a key player in all things concerning your goals.

Excuses never produced any results, so aim to look for opportunities even amid despair. Adversity is only but a temporary setback, a chance to strengthen your mental and physical resilience to come back stronger. Next time you encounter a setback just remember that "A setback is a setup for a comeback" – Willie Jolley. When you shift your mentality from a victim to a conqueror and take control of your destiny. Regardless of any internal or external influences, you will become unstoppable, a force to be reckoned with. Control what happens in and around you and not the other way around.

My late pastor Jason Steele often said that "positioning and environment are crucial to each person's success." It is imperative to evaluate your environment as regularly as possible, this way, you will allow yourself the necessary growth for your next step or destination. W. Clement Stone said, "You are a product of your environment. So, choose the environment that will best develop you toward your objective." Not only that but having the right people in your life is a sure way to getting to where you need to be, you need people that will cheer you on and support your dreams. Offer you candid and honest constructive criticism. I suggest that you do all that is necessary to bring your goal and ideas to fruition. It will not fall on your lap simply because it is destined for you. And remember, hard work is not a prerequisite for achieving your purpose or vision. You have to work smart.

In the summer of 2017 during a holiday to Zante in Greece, I woke up early one morning to prepare breakfast, I was getting ready to fry some eggs when I started looking for a pan. I opened the cupboard where I noticed a big pot and a small pan, I took up the pot and as soon as I did this I saw a sticker on the side of the pot and it showed that this particular pot was able to withstand 200 degrees heat. Out of interest, I checked out the cooker and it only had 3 dials which are equivalent to heat of 90 degrees Celsius.

Immediately, I thought to myself "This pot had the potential to be used for far more, but because of the 90 degrees limit – it could only ever function at 90 degrees Celsius in that environment." Using this analogy, to flourish and thrive as an individual, you need to be in the right place and know that not all environments are conducive to your growth.

In an environment that is instrumental to your growth, there's always someone who has the knowledge and expertise you need to attain the next stage of your greatness. If you do not align yourself to be where they are, you will simply stall and eventually get frustrated. Finally, a journey that should have taken you a month ends up taking years, and not because of your incompetence but because you're situated in the wrong place. I agree that the environment does not always determine your trajectory or where you end up in life because a flower has the potential to grow on stones as well. However, imagine another flower growing in rich soil, which flower do you think has a better shot at being all that it can be? I believe that it is crucial to ensure that you are surrounded by like-minded people and shaping your environment into one that kindles and fosters success. We don't come from the same background evidently, nor do we have the same start in life. Some of us come from broken families, poverty-stricken homes, while others have a much better start. I certainly do not come from a wealthy background, but my parents did what they could with what they had to raise me and my siblings. Now, just because I grew up not having everything I needed should not mean that I can't change my story. While my parents did what they could with what they had, the onus is now on me to take the mantle and shape the future I envisage and want to see. I am ultimately responsible for my life, and I must place myself in positions of success, and all this starts with my environment and the people I keep around me.

In life, you won't always find yourself in the most ideal situations. I suggest you make sacrifices for the greater good where necessary. Most of all, learn to develop the ability to adapt to various scenarios. Failure to do this is a simple recipe for disaster, and you will find yourself paying a hefty price along the line. Those that invest their time in personal growth, and focus their attention on becoming their best versions, are the ones who will reap the harvest. Always bear in mind that your success is not dependent on your convenience, but it will create comfort for you.

There's a saying that "A shark kept in a fish tank will only grow up to 8ft, but a shark in the ocean has the potential to grow over 8ft." The moral of the story here is that it is impossible to outgrow the environment that you are in if you do not change the way that you think. Your environment is not only limited to a geographical location, But It can also include the people you keep around you. You cannot be around small-thinking people and expect that you will yield a different result. You need to be selfish about who, and what you let into your space. This is what separates successful people from unsuccessful ones. Do not let anyone with an inferior complex and small thinking tendency into your space. Chaplain Ronnie Melancon said, "Show me your friends, and I'll show you your future." This statement couldn't be farther from the truth– You see people are always saying something, the question is whom you will listen to. More often than not, these are traits that can be adopted through spending enough time in someone's presence. Solomon, the wisest man to walk this earth, wrote in Proverbs 13:20 that: "He that walks with wise men shall be wise: but a companion of fools shall be destroyed." Similarly, in 1 Corinthians 15:33, it says that "Bad company corrupts good character."

Growth is inevitable when you are in the right environment, adjust and re-evaluate your situation and the influences around you as often as you can. Jim Rohn once said: "You are the average of the five people you spend most of your time with." Choose carefully, your success depends on it!

Take for instance the process of pruning a plant, it involves the horticultural and silvicultural practice. In short silvicultural is the process of removing selective parts of the plant such as deadwood, damaged, diseased, and any unwanted, or structurally unsound parts of the plant like branches, roots, and buds. This process then allows for the plant to improve and grow healthily. Horticultural on the other hand is the process of growing the plants, from adding manure to giving them the right nutrients as well as watering the plants. The two go hand in hand, you cannot just prune and not maintain afterward.

It is clear to see from the description above that even we as human beings have a crucial role to play when it comes to helping ourselves. You must empty the excess water seeping into the boat, or else you will drown. The next chapter will delve deeper into the subject of the environment.

Action Points to Achieve Productivity & Eliminate Excuses

- The first step is honesty, realising that excuses are lies. This can extend to relationships if you are not interested in going out for food be honest with your friend, if you are procrastinating be honest with yourself and make an action plan on how to achieve your goal/s.

- Be intentional about wanting to succeed – create a vision board and a to-do list for each day, every week, and every month. Analyse these every day to see what you have achieved and where you need to improve.

- Prioritise acting on bigger activities right down to the smaller ones in an expeditious way. There is no point putting off what

35

you can do today for tomorrow as this will only increase your load. After all, it was Pablo Picasso that said, "Only put off until tomorrow what you are willing to die having left undone."

- Prioritise your time effectively by utilizing your talents and resources to achieve your desired results. Remove yourself from friendships and relationships that are draining the energy in your life. Take steps to improve yourself in areas that are important to you.

Associates, Acquaintances, and Your Environment – Where you see yourself vs where you are today.

CHAPTER V

"A little yeast works through the whole batch of dough."
—Galatians 5:9

The environment is one of the most important aspects for anything or anyone to grow, yet an aspect that continues to be ignored by many. I tend to spend a considerable amount of time at home on days when I am not working, and I discovered that when the house has not been cleaned, my creativity becomes stifled. All the clutter whether it be the dishes in the sink, the clothes that need washing, or ironing and folding. I am generally a smart person but, there are times when things may be out of place, and it is in these moments that I can decide to either continue working in the mess or I can decide to create a tranquil and peaceful environment. The latter is of course the ideal scenario, by so doing I allow myself to be productive all at once. In the same vein, imagine a jug full of water, the moment you pour a dash of red squash, the water will start to turn red even though there's more water than the squash.

By the same token, have you ever noticed that when you place a rotten fruit in a batch of good fruit, it will debase the rest of the fruits, and quickly? However, if you remove the rotten apple from the equation suddenly, you've paved the way for the rest of the good apples to blossom and last longer. In the same way, being around toxic people has the same effect on your life, therefore make sure that you are always aware of your surroundings and environment. It is impossible to be in an environment and not be influenced. You'll inevitably start observing some traits and even displaying similar mannerisms and ways of behaviour.

You must create the environment you want and desire. You must visualize what you want, write it down, and put it on a vision board to observe and make that desire a reality within your mental space. Anything or idea formed inside the brain eventually manifests itself in the physical form. My late pastor Jason Steele often said that "Your external manifestation is a direct reflection of your internal thoughts." Allow yourself to be in places that induce positive thoughts so that you can visualize and create your ideal environment, first through thoughts, then physically.

I recall watching a short video documenting the Global Cheese Awards. The camera panned across to a table, on this table was a gentleman called Steve. Steve owned a farm in Scotland, he attended these awards annually for many years. I listened as Steve told some of his industry peers something that stuck out to me; he said: "I've got a degree in disappointment." This got me thinking, how he was going to win in the first place when he had given himself a degree in failure. His thoughts became what limited him, and this line of thinking can never produce anything positive.

If you stay in a dirty room long enough, it will start to feel comfortable. Similarly, staying in a job that does not stimulate you will only stall your growth. Even more alarming is the fact that familiarity can eventually convince you that this is the best thing that has ever happened to you. It goes without saying then that if you stay in toxic friendships long enough. You will accept it as part of your life, and your growth will be jeopardised. I think you get my point now, so it is imperative to ensure that you declutter as often as you can in your life. Re-evaluate, re-assess, and reposition.

I injured my lower back in 2012 while helping my friend lift large speakers for an event. The next day I felt a sharp pain in my left leg, which eventually spread to my right leg, It was the most excruciating pain I had ever experienced in my life. I struggled to sleep most nights and had to consult a physiotherapist who told me that I had sciatica. As you can imagine, I was displeased to hear this as I had always maintained a healthy lifestyle with regular gym attendance. Suddenly, I had this pain that rendered me weak and unable to do all the activities that I used to do freely. Some strong antibiotics (Co-Codamol) were prescribed to help me combat the pain and sleep at night.

I underwent many physiotherapy sessions, and they never seemed to help, only giving me temporary easement to my joints and back. Over time, however, I learned to live with this pain, and it became my routine, unfortunately. I stopped going to the gym entirely, I became miserable and in constant pain. I had accepted the reality that I would always be in pain, I stopped attempting to get rid of it. However, as time went by, I began challenging the way that I thought. I stopped feeling sorry for myself and refused to let the pain I was going through become the norm by taking control of my life. I had to step up and do unique things, I had to get back to the gym, and that I did. As soon as I did this, my body began to feel great again, albeit a struggle initially due to the pain I had on my lower back.

Today I am much happier and glad that I stepped up when I did by refusing to settle for a life of self-pity and pain. Do things today that will create a brighter tomorrow for you. Make decisions that will not make you have a regretful tomorrow. Use your time wisely and have no regrets in the grand scheme of things. I continuously remind myself that the difference between a successful individual and me is a simple application, action, and execution. Time remains the most significant currency we all share. We have the same amount regardless of age, gender, and race. Start with a single step! That is what this book echoes. We all have 86400 seconds, 1440 minutes, 24 hours a day. In each week, we all have 604800 seconds, 10080 minutes, and 168 hours, each passing moment is irrecoverable. Ultimately, missed opportunities become yesterday's regrets and mistakes, resulting in 'Shoulda, woulda, coulda.'

Aim to create new experiences always, this way, you will continue to grow and challenge the status quo. Take time to appreciate your achievements, for where gratitude lies, there are immeasurable blessings and contentment. Acknowledge your results, but do not let yesterday's accomplishments stop you from aiming higher. Your achievements must propel you to even greater heights and further than you can fathom. Ellen Johnson Sirleaf said, "If your dreams do not scare you, then they are not big enough." Similarly, Kevin "Kevin Gates" Gilyard echoed this sentiment when he said that "The scariest thing in the world is following your dreams."

It is not surprising when Les Brown said that "Most people fail in life not because they aim too high and miss, but because they aim too low and hit." So, "make no small plans for they have no magic to stir men's blood" – Daniel Burnham. I say it is time to step up, become a person of action. I firmly believe that if people put the same effort, and dedication they invest in their 9-5-day jobs, they can make their dreams come true. There is a lot that can be achieved in their own lives. I am not saying that jobs are a bad thing, but they can be detrimental to the person that has a vision of where they want to go in life.

Vision is a crucial driver to where you want to be in life, thus the saying "A man without a vision is already at his destination," is true for many people. It is no wonder then that Lewis Carroll said that "If you don't know where you are going, any road will get you there." In everything that you do, make sure that this does not become your reality – instead aim to be a high achiever and set goals regularly. You can break this down into small achievable tasks throughout the month and start to chip away at your targets one step at a time.

A lot of people go to work between the hours of 9 in the morning and 5 in the evening, day-in-day-out, and forget to invest time in their business outside of work. You must not neglect your goal and help others achieve theirs. It is vital to pursue the things that you are passionate about. You need to make time for personal projects at every opportunity you get. Use the time you have after work to practice the guitar, write that business plan, strategize, and study. Substitute things that don't add value to your life and replace them with the important ones. Turn off the television to study, shun partying for planning and strategizing for that business you have always wanted to start. Don't get me wrong everything has a time and a place, as such a balance must be struck between leisure and work. Balance is paramount to everything you do in life since too much of anything is not healthy. No matter how good a thing is - one must approach every situation with due care and discipline.

> *"Too many of us are not living our dreams because we are living our fears."*
>
> - LES BROWN

If you are to experience success and true wins, then you must think like a winner. You must apply what is called the 'I Am Factor'; a phrase coined by the great Bishop Tudor Bismark of Zimbabwe. The idea being that to attract anything to your life, you need to place the words 'I Am' before any statement. Creating an environment of success depends on what you say, of course after 'I Am.' Whatever you place after I Am will manifest itself in your life, it becomes an affirmation. If you say, "I am successful," then everything in the success arena starts looking for you. And if you were to say, "I am poor" – then everything in the poor-universe will search you out in all its glory. So then, do not be surprised when things happen to you whether negative or positive, instead, evaluate what you did right or wrong and correct your mental attitude. If indeed, what you have attracted is positive, then continue in that vein of positive thought. Do your best to maintain a positive mindset, cultivate an environment and habit of appreciating what you have and how far you have come. This will create an environment of gratitude, which is paramount to maintaining a positive outlook on life. Create an atmosphere of success through your words, start confessing positive affirmations and words in your life. You can say things like "I am wealthy, I influence my generation, I am the head and not the tail, above only and not beneath, I am intelligent." You can add more to these to make it more personal to you. If you set aside time each day to say these things to yourself, you will notice over time that these things will start to sound and be a part of who you are.

Someone once said that "If you hang around the barbershop long enough, you'll eventually get a haircut." The significance of this is self-explanatory; visualize your ideal lifestyle, frequent the places you would like to own or be a part of eventually. Keep the type of friends around you that possess the aptitude and attributes you would like to one day possess. It may sound insane but if you want a house worth a million pounds then book a viewing and go and view, book that test drive of your dream car. There's a shift that begins to take place in your psyche that tells you that this is possible, do this long enough and you will start to attract these things to your life. Have you ever noticed that once you become interested in something, for example, a particular car model? You start to see it more than usual, not because there's an influx of the car model suddenly. But because you have allowed that car into your environment and now you seem to spot it every other minute?

Living A Purpose-Driven Life: The mental attitude it takes to not live a mediocre life.

CHAPTER VI

The mystery of human existence lies not in just staying alive, but finding something to live for"
– Fyodor Dostoyevsky

A plumber does not quit the profession because another plumber is overcharging, providing a terrible service, and putting the profession in disrepute. That plumber has a choice to become a good example and provide the best service. In like manner. One lousy crop does not represent the whole farm. In simple terms, just because there are corrupt politicians doesn't mean you have to give up your dream of becoming one. If you are called to that arena, go and serve diligently and leave an indelible mark on your generation and oncoming ones. In the same vein, a police officer would be amiss if they quit because another officer abuses the law. Become the best that you can be, become a prime example, and a leader in your field of expertise, do everything with excellence. I am unashamedly a man of faith, I am reminded of Colossians 2:23, where it says, "Whatever you do, work heartily, as for the Lord and not for men."

Similarly, Titus 2:7 says, "Show yourself in all aspects to be a model of good works, and in your teaching show integrity, dignity."

Considering this, be the kind of person others can count on as a great example of success and best practice in your field of expertise. Do not succumb to mediocrity, you were made to be great. The late Nelson Mandela said, "Our deepest fear is not that we are weak, our deepest fear is that we are powerful beyond measure." It is our light, not our darkness that most frightens us. We ask ourselves, who am I to be brilliant, gorgeous, talented, and fabulous? who are you not to be? You are a child of God". You must be willing to take a stand, decide on what it is you stand for. Only then, will you know what you need to do to achieve your goals because ultimately your "Playing small does not serve the world ... As we are liberated from our fear, our presence automatically liberates others", - Marianne Williamson. Do not allow yourself to shrink in the presence of others so that they don't feel inferior around you. Create an environment and attitude of change, one that inspires those around you to have no choice but to change for the better. Maintain the spirit of excellence that exudes from your demeanour. If people you keep around you do not excel, you are not doing enough. Let your excellence be contagious, nothing speaks volumes like evidence, don't just talk it, walk it. You must not only talk the talk but walk the walk, in other words, actions speak louder than words, for they are your voice expressed in practice.

The best way to tell people is to show them, arguably it shouldn't be this way, but people are, after all, visual beings – hence the popularly used phrase "seeing is believing." Anything that is presented with a compelling visual usually gets people more stimulated than what is solely offered in text format. According to Edgar Dale's Cone of Experience, people remember 10% of what they read, 20% of what they hear, and 50% of what they see and hear. Your work should speak for itself, let it be near impossible for your field of interest to be discussed without your name being mentioned in the conversation. When you think of influential musicians, the likes of Beyoncé, Prince, or Madonna spring to mind. Let alone, prominent politicians of all time – you are likely to mention Nelson Mandela, Barack Obama, Winston Churchill, to name but a few. All these individuals have certain things such as consistency and excellence in their fields in common. For example, Madonna is regarded as a marketing and transformational genius for being able to adapt to changes and apply herself to the evolving audiences and musical styles throughout the decades. The likes of Nelson Mandela and Barack Obama are known to have changed the course of history, throughout the political arena. It is well documented that Nelson Mandela spent 27 years in prison. His prison sentence was split between Robben Island, Pollsmoor, and Victor Verster Prison, respectively. It was his desire for equality between people of colour and the white people that made officials incarcerate him.

Nelson Mandela fought against the apartheid regime to liberate all the marginalised and ill-treated South Africans. The apartheid-era made it illegal for both blacks and whites to mix, interact, and even share amenities such as toilets. Upon his release in 1990, he became a beacon of hope for many South Africans. Going on to become South Africa's first black president, a milestone shared with Barack Obama who became the first black president in the United States of America in 2008. Nelson Mandela's capacity to forgive his oppressors, and seek a better and more inclusive South Africa made him an incredible figure and humanitarian.

I believe that you too can change the course of history if only you will listen to the voice that is within. I believe that your destiny is tied into somebody else's and as such procrastinating and shying away from your goals is doing you and other people a lot of disservices. Every time you fail to exercise your God-given gift, you are depriving yourself and others of benefiting and sharing in your gift. After all, our desires, dreams, and aspirations are most fulfilled when we help others. There is always an opportunity to gain in helping someone else. We sit on chairs today that someone made, beds that someone dreamed into reality. We eat all kinds of foods because someone saw the need to plant, grow, and harvest. It is no wonder Zig Ziglar said, "You can get everything you want in life if you will just help enough people to get what they want." The key to success is the desire to find out what people need and then finding a way to cater to that need. There is no way on God's green earth that you will be poor if you help other people achieve their needs. Warren Buffet echoed this notion when he said, "Someone's sitting in the shade today because someone planted a tree a long time ago."

I am sure that we can all agree that success is attractive, regardless of where it is derived. What I mean, for example, is I am not a big basketball fan. However, it does not mean I can't appreciate the art of the sport. You might not be a basketball fan, but the moment you watch a game with the likes of Lebron James, or Steph Curry, you are bound to be on the edge of your seat. These players possess pristine excellence, and you do not need to understand the rules or the sport to notice that they play exceptionally well. It is often said that your gift will make room for you and this is very true. When you walk in your gifting, it will open doors you did not know existed. For example, some celebrities have perfumes, aftershave lines, clothing brands, and many more business endeavours which were not their primary aim. They focused single-handedly on being the best in their respective fields. From Michael Jordan investing more hours into practising his basketball skills when all the other players went home, to Beyoncé's determination to become the best music artist and performer, she can be. This determination and excellence in their craft opened doors for new ventures, which were only possible after they had dominated their respective spheres and areas of influence. Michael Jordan started the famous Jordan line with Nike, an enterprise that has generated more than a billion-dollar. To this day, Jordan's are statement trainers for athletes, actors, and the consumer market at large. In short, "It is never too late to be what you might have been." George Elliot

Always remember that playing small does not serve the world whatsoever . . . "As we are liberated from our fear, our presence automatically liberates others." Marianne Williamson

You need to take risks, and make great strides to achieve your dreams, take every opportunity to learn, and seize every moment that propels you to greatness. It would be a pity for the world to never benefit from what you could have accomplished. If only dreams could speak from the grave, I am confident that we would be astonished at how many are there but never fulfilled. It is no wonder then that "The wealthiest places in the world are not gold mines, oil fields, diamond mines, or banks. The wealthiest place is by far the cemetery, for there lie businesses that were never started, masterpieces that were never painted . . . buried in the cemetery is the greatest treasure of untapped potential." – Myles Munroe. Aim to empty yourself of every gift and talent that you possess. Unfortunately, sometimes, the sad passing of someone is when people start to reflect on their impact and what they are doing with their lives. Bronnie Ware, a renowned author from Australia popularly known for the book 'The Top Five Regrets of the Dying: A Life Transformed by the Dearly Departing.' Talks about the many regrets she often heard uttered by those she cared for in palliative care. These patients spent between three to six weeks of their lives with Bronnie before they went home to die.

The top five regrets of the dying according to Bronnie were as follows;

1. "I wish I'd dared to live a life true to myself, not the life others expected of me."

This is true, living for other people's approval and acceptance is a losing game, it is an impossible task. Trying to please others can only end one way, and that is this, "If you live for their acceptance, you will die from their rejection" – Lecrae Moore

It is no secret that each one of us has a purpose in this lifetime. A purpose so unique to each individual that it cannot be duplicated. I once overheard someone say that "You make a perfect original, but a terrible copy" – Author Unknown. It is easy to fall prey to the expectations of our loved ones, especially our parents, or relatives. It can seem like everyone knows what is best for you at every turn sometimes. For example, Florence Nightingale the lady that changed the course of modern-day nursing and left an indelible mark on society. At the age of 16 years old, she had decided that she would pursue nursing, a career that was looked down upon because of its reputation. In addition, her parents also detested Florence's career choice greatly because they wanted her to follow the Victorian standards that placed importance on marriage and childbearing. Florence changed the course of history by introducing improved sanitary conditions in hospitals and developed better nursing practices, including her instrumental role in passing legislation that would force extant buildings to connect with the main drainage. The results were outstanding, increasing Britain's life expectancy by 20 years in 1935. Her Majesty Queen Victoria was a big fan of her work.

Miles Davis, the nine-time Grammy award winner might have never turned out to be whom we know today as the greatest jazz musician of all time had he pursued a career playing the violin instead of the trumpet because according to his mother, it was a lot more socially accepted in a segregated community. On the other hand, his father wanted him to be a dentist.

Ironically, isn't it interesting that both Florence and Miles have this one thing in common, in that their parents were thinking about what would be socially accepted, more than what both Miles and Florence were interested in pursuing? Whilst parents may have the best intentions for their children, it is important that everyone can make their own informed decisions. I remember having a conversation with my father and he randomly asked me "My son, why don't you enrol in medical school? and my response was simple "I don't like blood, I loathe its sight." It was probably an innocent question, but these types of questions have a lasting impression because they can make you feel as though you are not doing enough in your parent's eyes. It is therefore important to free yourself from these expectations in order to thrive and dare to live a life that is pleasing to you and is in full pursuit of your purpose.

2. "I wish I didn't work so hard."

The term 'Work Hard, Play Hard' is often thrown around so carelessly, and while this may seem like an extreme expression. There is a key lesson to be gleaned from this phrase. There must be a balance to everything that we do in life, whilst we aspire to be productive, it is essential to have a great work-life balance. Work smart and not hard, so that you can make time for the vital things in life. Master using your time more efficiently always. I suggest that you carry out your most difficult tasks early in the day whilst your brain is still fresh, this way you can tackle the easier task towards the end of your day to allow yourself much-needed rest. Plan for your annual leave and change environments where possible to allow your brain to recalibrate.

3. "I wish I'd dared to express my feelings."

Genuine and real friends will appreciate an honest person who is not afraid to express exactly how they feel. If your group of friends only like you when you agree with them. Then they are not real, find yourself friends that will appreciate and encourage your truth. You might have heard the phrase 'Truth Hurts', as true as this might be, it is also true that truth heals. It can deal with the inner struggles of our souls. Ultimately it comes down to this, you cannot change something that you are not willing to confront. It is no wonder then that I often hear the saying "The truth will set you free". I suggest that you become as honest with yourself as possible, this way you can manage your and other people's expectations. The person that you like may well be waiting for you to make the first move, so express yourself. That potential business partner or friend may just be waiting for you to make the first move, so go for it!

4. "I wish I had stayed in touch with my friends."

I believe in the idea that "No Man Is an Island", what this means is that you cannot do this thing we call life on your own, it is impossible. You need those people around you who are there to lift you when you are down, and equally, you can help them up in their time of need. Find people you can share and create moments and memories with, after all the African proverb sums it up perfectly "Umuntu ngumuntu, ngabantu", meaning a human being is a human because of others. Another proverb says "Izandla ziyagezana", directly translated, hands wash each other. Simply put, this proverb alludes to the fact that you may help me today, but tomorrow I may be in the position to help you. Reminiscent of the "You scratch my back and I scratch your back" idiom.

Three friends that are real, honest, and supportive, are far much better than ten friends who only want to be around you for what you can do for them. I suggest you find yourself, consistent friends, maintain those relationships. Just as you water plants, water those relationships, and make sure that they help you to become a better version of yourself and vice versa.

5. "I wish that I had let myself be happier."

It is easy to get caught up in the rat race of life, trying to accumulate things. In your busy schedule, find time to look after yourself and make sure that you create a happy environment. Look at yourself smile in the mirror, it is the most magically beautiful sight you'll ever see.

I want you to understand that this life we live is not a rehearsal, you will not get another chance to relive it. Therefore, choose to spend your time wisely on things of value, live a purposefully driven life.

Dr. Howard Thurman made an interesting observation, one that I am sure most would find idealistic and relatable. He says, "The ideal situation for any man or woman to die is to have family members standing with them as they cross over." . . . Imagine, "If you will, being on your death-bed, and standing around your bed are the ghosts of ideas, the abilities, the talents, the gifts, the dreams given to you by life, that you, for whatever reason, never pursued. Imagine them saying we came to you, and only you could have given us life, and now we must die with you forever." – Dr. Howard Thurman. The moral of the story is, make sure that your dreams do not die with you. Eliminate procrastination, and curve that voice that tells you, "You are not good enough," you are powerful beyond measure, you are the epitome of excellence, and you are success personified. Speak these words to yourself, you are your biggest cheerleader, you are your most significant asset. Remember that yesterday is gone, today is a gift, and tomorrow is a blessing. Neither of us knows what tomorrow holds, we only know what yesterday had in store. One thing we do know for sure is what is happening right now. Even so, we do not know what will happen an hour from now, considering this, we must fully utilize every moment at our disposal. This recurring theme on the importance of time should highlight to you just how vital of a topic it is, it transcends into all spheres of our lives. Master your time, and you are halfway to your dreams.

Will Smith was right when he said that "God placed the best things in life on the other side of terror." So, next time you see a challenge, you must see an opportunity instead of the impending number of issues that might be ahead. The only thing you should be thinking about is the reward and what tools you need to succeed. Remember that "Our next level always lives on the other side of our biggest fear" – Dean Graziosi.

> *"The purpose of life is to live a life of Purpose".*
>
> – RICHARD HEIDER

Preparation Is The First Step Towards Your Purpose

CHAPTER VII

"Make no small plans for they have no magic to stir men's blood"

It was Abraham Lincoln that said, "Give me six hours to chop down a tree and I will spend the first four sharpening the axe." Similarly, Benjamin Franklin once famously said that "By failing to prepare, you are preparing to fail."

In my own life, there are many instances where I have often failed to prepare, thinking back to my university years at Loughborough University particularly. I wanted to do well in my Tourism Management course, but when it came down to preparation for exams and assignments, I often found myself playing catch up at the very last minute. I would not study for exams until the week before I was due to sit, I would do my assignments at the last minute. This finally caught up with me in my final year and I found myself struggling to keep up with my workload. I passed my course but with subpar results.

It is clear as day that preparation plays a very important role in our lives, one that is not to be taken lightly. I mean imagine going through life on chance, how chaotic would that be? I firmly believe that preparing and planning bring order to your life, it will act as a guiding compass to your path. Planning and preparing enhance your vision, and as your vision enhances, so does your ability to achieve it, for how can you achieve what you cannot envision? It is a fact of life that to make something of your life, you must make a conscious decision to effectively plan, prepare, and execute.

The lack of preparation as I have come to find out will always have a hefty cost attached to it, with interest. It is better to be prepared at all times, this way when an opportunity arises, you can seize the moment. There's a saying that "If you stay ready, you don't have to get ready." I believe that this phrase is representative of someone who possesses consistency and approaches life with an attitude of a can-do mentality. Often people equate other people's successes to luck, but I believe that a lot of the time it is a case of opportunity meets preparation. Take, for instance, Michael Dapaah, who adopts the moniker 'Big Shaq,' it is no secret that Michael has been propelled to stardom by his viral video where he raps, "Mans not Hot" on the BBC1 Xtra radio show. A lot of people don't know that he has been actively doing comedy for many years dating back to 2014, the recorded year for his career start.

He appeared on the Charlie Sloth show and received rave reviews for his rapping clip, and upon witnessing this, he seized the moment and released a full track of titled 'Mans not Hot'. His music video currently has over 380 million views on YouTube, and he's traveled around the world as a result. I firmly believe that without any prior work in the background, he would have never had the opportunity to even appear on the Charlie Sloth show. It is clear to see how working in the dark eventually made room for him in the spotlight. So yes, preparation, when no one is watching, is what sets you up for success in the light. A lot of time and sacrifice spent in the dark, where only discipline and consistency are the key drivers and motivators, your character is refined and revealed at the same time. The truth is that the person that you are when no one else is watching is the real you, can you carry on when the burden gets heavy? Can you persevere when it looks like the odds are against you? Can you continue to hope amid disarray? Ultimately, that is the difference between winners and losers. Winners hold on to a hope that in the end, they will see the light of day, this type of people understand the principles guiding the grinding out of results. If they want to get the six-pack they desperately need, they know it is vital to sacrifice time and be disciplined in the gym. Even when the going gets tough, they will keep pushing on, and if need be, they have to forego certain foods that might adversely affect the development of the six-pack they desire.

- If you have ever had the misfortune of locking your car keys inside your car, then you know how costly it can be. Expect to pay anything between £200 to upwards of £500. I had to find out the hard way when I accidentally locked my keys in my car once. I had no choice, so I had to pay up – mistakes can be very costly.

All these things are somewhat related to a lack of preparation and perhaps not paying enough attention to the essential elements, the two go hand in hand. There are plenty of benefits in planning and development, some of these includes;

- No unnecessary expenses.
- Full and total awareness of what's to come.
- Peace of mind.
- Feel in total control
- Effective use of time and resources.

Planning is very important for it prepares you for success. Keep in mind, however, that whilst planning is very important, making small plans because you are scared is equally as detrimental. I am reminded of Daniel Burnham when he said, "Make no small plans for they have no magic to stir men's blood."

It is better to stay ready so that you don't have to wait when the right opportunity presents itself. A champion does not get created the moment they win the race, but rather, it's the seconds, minutes, hours, days, weeks, months, and years of preparation invested in becoming the best. Race day is merely a display of all the hard work, blood, sweat, and tears the winner has endured, a day to claim the prize for which you have worked hard to achieve by planning your time. Prepared people approach life's challenges with anticipation, but those who fail to adopt this trait, approach challenges with a defeated mindset.

Finding beauty in the struggle: Overcoming fear and using struggle as fuel

CHAPTER VIII

"Make no small plans for they have no magic to stir men's blood"

It would appear to me that fear has a hierarchical order. If pain is unpleasant, then why can two people have two completely different experiences with a hot curry? You may discover that one of the two people experience great agony and pain from the curry, while the other thoroughly enjoyed it. Thus, when you begin to reconceptualize anything that would ordinarily induce pain and grief and see it as a challenge, you begin to feel accomplished. The reason you may feel accomplished is that you would have demonstrated strength and self-control for yourself and others. You need to stop looking at pain as a threat.

Pain can be a blessing in disguise, therefore, choose to see the reward on the other side of pain. Ultimately, pain not only challenges us, but it presents us with the opportunity to strengthen and grow our wings and character, for "Suffering produces perseverance; 4 perseverance, character; and character, hope. 5 And hope does not put us to shame" – Romans 5:3-5.

Growing up, I always heard the phrase, "No pain, no gain" uttered by a lot of athletes, and now that I am an adult, I understand that most leaders adhere to this concept. There are a lot of benefits that can be yielded from pain, these include the following;

- You can develop strength from pain as I said above.

- It can act as an indicator that something requires our attention.

- It can bring about a change for the good as a result of highlighting an issue (which by now you should be referring to as a challenge) and you acting on it.

- - It can bring people together because one way or the other all humans experience a type of pain on this life journey.

- - Pain can make you appreciate the times when you had no pain, which in turn can keep you content and appreciative.

- - Grief allows us to learn, grow, as well as improve our skills.

- - It increases your endurance and ability to withstand challenges, as well as increase your capacity and patience.

- - Finally, it allows you to have sympathy for others who might be going through pain.

People who achieve excellent results in every sphere they are involved in have mastered this thing we call fear. I often hear the phrase "Success is addictive," so no wonder after they have discovered the best on the other side of terror. They are striving for more, and while this may seem insane and risky to the average person, they forge ahead and take new risks every single day. In other words, they are risk-averse in more ways than one.

I went away for two weeks as part of a study clinic in 2018, I found myself with a group of guys, all total strangers. There was a variety of activities to keep us entertained, including table tennis, X-box, DVDs and a pool table amongst others.

A group of 6 other guys and I decided to play the pool table on one of the days, and we would go on to play most days. I consider myself an outstanding pool table player having played since I was 7 years old. I would stay at my local games club as late as midnight sometimes. I would be on a winning streak the whole night at times until someone knocked me out at which point I would go home. The club was less than 200 yards from my house, so I felt safe even during late nights as a student.

As soon as I met the six guys I knew I had it in me to pretty much win against every person there, I won a few games for the first two days. In the days that followed, I found myself challenged by a guy called Maury, whom I lost to a few games, and soon a few became every game. Leon and Ryan, on the other hand, were able to win against Maury several times. I wondered how it was possible to keep winning against Ryan and Leon only to lose to Maury. I soon realized that mentally, I had disqualified myself before I even started playing Maury. As soon as I knew it was his turn, it was as if I'd admitted defeat. And sure, enough without fail, I was losing continuously. On the same token, Leon would occasionally say "I keep losing" each time before he played me. He had no confidence in his ability to win against me. Because of this, I already had the upper hand, and I was able to dominate him consistently.

As the days went on, I decided to take a break from playing pool to gather my thoughts. I came back with a better perspective, I even managed to score a few wins against Maury. This time I could tell that each time I won against him, he was beginning to lose his confidence, and as he did that, I gained mine instead. He started missing apparent balls he'd usually score in previous games, this made me aware that perspective is everything. Once you show any sign of fear towards your opponent or challenge that you're facing, you've given the opponent or challenge a better chance and position to dominate you.

More often than not, the thing that is standing between you and success is that very idea of inadequacy, feeling sorry for yourself, disqualifying yourself before you've even started. Having a defeated mindset when approaching a competition is just as well a defeat, without the necessity of action or participation. The moment you speak to the giant in your mind, you awaken everything that belongs to the realm of possibilities. Whenever you find yourself in challenging situations, it is very crucial to affirm and confess positive words to yourself. As I carried on playing pool, I started to speak words of affirmation to myself. "I'm the best there is, and this game is mine to win," needless to say, the moment I did this, the results were phenomenal, I could hear Leon saying, "Dave's back." What had happened initially in the previous week is that I had won numerous games, and this same winning streak was back.

Ultimately, you have to develop a winning mentality, create room for your success by the words you say to yourself. When all is said and done, what matters is what you say to yourself.

Here are a few ways in which fear work for you;

1. Wisdom - In a somewhat bizarre manner, fear can instil wisdom in you, by learning to adapt to various situations and control your emotions. You can gain irrepressible knowledge, it helps you navigate a space whereby you are out of your comfort zone.

2. Motivator - Fear will motivate you to accomplish a seemingly tough feat set before you. The fear of failure can push you to newer heights. Sometimes, this can be induced by peer pressure when you want to feel good about yourself and impress your friends, etc.

3. Result driver - Fear can also work as an incentive driver, it can challenge you to prove it wrong. Achieving things you never thought possible could incentivise you to continue striving to do even riskier or once fearsome activities.

4. Competitor driver - Fear often drives the spirit of competition, this could range from that sky diving or even skiing activity you've always wanted to do. For some, it is a simple phobia of spiders, snakes, or even heights. Conquering this can boost your confidence and competitive spirit.

5. Protection from danger - Fear has the potential to protect you from danger; inadvertently, it could act like the gut instinct that tells you about a threat that is coming or associated with a particular activity. However, it is essential not to let this type of protection from danger stop you from attempting anything. This can easily disable you from ever attempting anything at all - which will mean you are jailed by your fear.

Remember that only people that take risks reap the rewards. Stephen Hunt said it best when he said that "If you're not living on the edge, you're taking up too much space." This simply means that you must be willing and able to take risks and not let fear derail you from doing all you can. Ultimately, fear is an invalid, inadequate feeling that tries to make itself valid. Richard Branson once used the phrase "Get comfortable with the uncomfortable, once you do, you'll find that you're living at a more exhilarating pace."

Develop a positive outlook on life: Overcoming the victim mentality

> *"Never feel sorry for yourself because no one owes you anything."*

To progress in life, you have to ditch the victim mentality, which says why me? Why does it always happen to me? To name a few. The question should be, why not you? People tend to become victims of their own words, feeling sorry for yourself does not change the situation nor make it better. It is vital not to let anything dictate how you feel and behave. It does not matter how fearful you are about where your next meal or paycheque is coming from. Whether you'll get that job, or get admitted to study that course you really want. The main thing is what you do in between and your attitude towards the situation. Speak positively and reposition yourself for success by thinking like you already have those things. Tune out the noise and say some positive affirmations each morning and throughout the day. Immediately you do this, you'll notice a change in how you feel and your attitude towards the things you desire.

Never feel sorry for yourself because no one owes you anything, always be ready to try another door. Don't wait idly for one opportunity to avail itself for you to be proactive. This way, you can never be at the mercy of anyone, but you'll always be able to move on if something does not work in your favour.

Those that invest in you when you have setbacks are the champions of your success and you should never forget them during your comeback season.

The Oxford dictionary defined fear as "An unpleasant emotion caused by the belief that someone or something is dangerous, likely to cause pain or a threat. It would appear to me that fear has a hierarchical order.

Terror, on the other hand, is defined as extreme fear, while being afraid, is classified as being frightened or nervous. Terror is at the ultimate end of the scale of fear, this explains why those that can exercise unparalleled boldness to go through those terrifying processes or situations always come out at the top. Successful people have mastered fear, in fact, they understand that fear is a doorway to success. I often hear the phrase, "Success is addictive," no wonder then, that after tasting success they never stop. They'll continue pushing even further, and this seems insane and risky to the average person.

Jump, build your wings on your way down: Living your life on the edge

"If you're not living on the edge, you're taking up too much space"
– Stephen Hunt

I dare say that a lot of people can see where their dreams and goals lie, but they are hanging onto the cliff that stands between them and their goals. More often than not, the best way to achieve your goal is to "jump off a cliff and build your wings on the way down" Ray Bradbury. I have come to the brutal realization that life happens and does not wait for any individual. I suggest you have a sense of urgency in attaining your goals, it is the biggest favour you can do for yourself. Do not mistake this with doing just about anything carelessly, what I mean here is that anything positive should not be overthought.

A lot of people do a lot of thinking and end up getting stuck with no action to back up what they are saying. If you have a business plan, or you have any other interests you would like to fulfil, do not wait for anyone to permit you. You are well within your capability and authority to act and achieve your goals. A lot of the time, what is stifling your progress is the perception that you are inexperienced, and the thought that you do not know where to start. The truth is that whether you are qualified or not, you can always learn, the only difference is your attitude towards your goal. Stop thinking that you need a lot of experience to pursue your dreams, what matters is that you start, you will learn along the way. There is no better way to learn than having guts and chutzpah. I will take you through a brief history of my career to help illustrate this for you. In 2018 I completed my MSc in quantity survey after spending prior years working in customer service roles. I was frustrated with where I was, and I knew deep down that there was a better career for me out there and upon reflection and self-evaluation I decided I was going to upskill myself. This paid off greatly because, by the time I had completed my studies I was offered a role with Highways England, I would go on to work in their commercial team dealing with high-level post-contract matters and managing projects with values up to £250m. Whilst others were content, I ensured that I learned my role at a greater speed to equip myself for my next move. At the beginning of January 2021, I started a new role as a Senior Cost Manager where I am effecting changes and implementing processes at a high level. It has taken me just over 2 years to get to this point, and I can't help but think what would have happened if I had decided not to step up and upskill myself out of fear, the only inevitable thing is time. I would have been regretting it had I not taken the plunge to apply for my MSc, and don't get me wrong this hasn't been without its challenges, I have had to overcome some of my greatest fears and face challenges along the way head-on.

You may not have an example of anyone successful in your family, but do not paint yourself with the brush of failure, even if where you come from is a harsh environment, do not let that determine your future. You can always rewrite the rules and challenge the status quo. You are your most powerful asset, and there's nothing you cannot do with unparalleled boldness and faith. Remember that whatever you do, and wherever you are "Failure is simply the opportunity to begin again, this time more intelligently," Henry Ford.

Your mind is a powerful tool that has the potential and ability to develop into something so amazing. You are worth it, don't say why me, instead why not you. You have every reason to be happy, every reason to reach your goals, go out, and work harder than ever. Sometimes the best thing you can do for yourself is to "Jump, and you'll build your wings on your way down." - Ray Bradbury. What this will do is enable you to fly eventually. You must want success more than breathing itself to succeed, we all know that if you swim underwater, you must come up to get some air because failing to do so could cause you to drown. Ultimately, it is your drive, passion, and determination that will open doors for you.

Turning wishes into actionable steps: Turn I wish, into I will

CHAPTER X

"Success won't happen in spite of you, but because of you"

The dictionary describes the term "I Wish" as "used with the past, simply to express that you feel sorry or sad about a state or situation that exists at the moment – or perhaps a particular action in the past."

Often, I hear people say things like, "I wish I were born in a wealthy family, I wish I were taller, I wish I were wealthy." They go on and on living in what I call "Wish land." I have sometimes found myself in situations where I am in denial about things that have happened in the past. Sometimes it is simply hard to accept things that have happened. When I was around 13 years old, I sustained a water burn across my chest following an attempt to make tea. I remember turning the kettle on as soon as I arrived home from school. We kept our kettle above the coal stove, as soon as the water had boiled - I reached over to pick it up, it slipped and burned me across my body. I became upset wishing my mother had moved out of the way as this led me to strain more than I should have.

I blamed everyone else but myself, but the truth is I should have been more careful. Your success depends on you and no one else, you are responsible for your life. I know that this statement is both challenging and exciting at the same time. Ultimately being responsible for your life requires discipline and a well-thought-out plan of execution to achieve your goals. In essence, success won't happen in spite of you, but because of you, so take control – you are the pilot, you are the chief executive officer, and the success of this company called 'You' depends on you. You are the director, and this film only stops when you say "cut". You are responsible for the product and no one else, everyone is part of the cast, but you determine the plot of this film.

The way I see it, we can wish for things to be different, or we can take charge of our lives and recognize that we are individuals first before we become a society. As such, all of us are not heading towards the same destination, neither can we all get to our goals using one prescribed method. Let's assume you are tolling the path of another person, I believe that even the person will always be a step ahead, because when and if you reach where they were yesterday. I assure you they have taken a few more steps, and by the time you get to where they were this year, they would have gone even further. So never get stuck in the rat race chasing the Joneses, carve out your path, and most importantly realize that this is not a sprint, but a marathon. Only the brave, bold, and courageous will survive, while others fall by the wayside. You have to make the essential decision of choosing to realize your full potential. Alternatively, don't copy others by following in the footsteps of originals who are living out their dreams and purposes. Remember that "You make a perfect original, but a poor copy." 'Author Unknown'

Spring into action

A lot of people procrastinate and delay for as long as possible before taking action in bids to get the perfect timing and for the stars to align, I have been guilty of this too in the past. With that said I have news for you, there is no such thing as the right time because you will always encounter new challenges or problems along the way. The best way to deal with this is to start anyway regardless of whether or not everything is aligned, as long as you have a plan you can make it work. It is Casey Neistat who said that *"The right time is always right now."*

5 Steps to ready you into action

1. Know and understand your why!

What motivates you to want to do what you want to do, because only then will you find the tenacity and the drive you need to push forward. The "why" will be your push when you hit a wall or a ceiling, it will be the key driver in getting you across the finish line. Without a good understanding of why you are doing something, it is frankly quite easy to give up because there is no purpose or bigger picture to what you are doing. Your why is your compass, without this, you might as well be wandering in the jungle and going around in circles.

2. Deal with your fears

To fully live out your dreams you must face your doubts and fears, after all, fear is the biggest killer of dreams in our generation and the ones that came before us. Fear has allowed a lot of dreams and goals to go unrealised. It is crucial to understand that there is beauty on the other side of fear, Will Smith once said that "Bliss is on the other side of fear." A lot of people are scared of living and taking leaps of faith because of fear of the unknown. You must

73

understand that fear is the thief that has the ability to keep you captive to your inferiority complex if you allow it. To fully realise your full potential, you must step up and do what you have never done before. Whenever you are faced with a challenge do not retreat, instead, seek ways of overcoming the challenge. It is vital to understand that there are no shortcuts to success, you can only conquer every insurmountable obstacle through perseverance and tenacity.

> *"...it took me 17 years and 114 days to become an OVERNIGHT SUCCESS."*
>
> - LIONEL MESSI.

3. Step out of your comfort zone

It has always been said that comfortability is the enemy of success, and I couldn't agree more with this statement. Complacency in its entirety is the perfect vehicle to achieving nothing. There is often a divide between complacency and contentment, a lot of people make the mistake of thinking that the two are the same thing, they are not! Simply put complacency can be described as one's refusal to improve, and often complacent people aren't happy with where they are, but they have no desire to do what is necessary to get to the next level because to them this is simply extra work and effort that they can do without. On the other hand, contentment is described as being happy, it could mean you are happy with what you have accomplished, or where you are in life and maybe the friendships you have formed. Contentment is good for progress because it allows you to reflect and look at where you have come from, where you are, and where you are going. As a result, you can practice appreciation and gratefulness, these are the ingredients required for progress in life.

> *"Remember if you are not living on the edge then you are taking up too much space."*
>
> – WILL WILLIS.

Imagine that your talents and gifts are on top of a mountain and the only way you can acquire them is by climbing to the top of this steep and high mountain. What would you do? Would you ignore their voice calling you day in and day out? Would you just look up at the mountain and say, "There are my gifts and talents at the top of the mountain", yet do nothing? Or would you do whatever it takes to climb that mountain? Would you not feel the urge to go and get what belongs to you? Yes, climbing the mountain would be tough, but then again nothing worthy just lands on your lap on a nice sunny day. You must have the tenacity and dedication needed to accomplish your goal, if you need to study, exercise, plan, whatever it is you need to reach your goals do it! It was Denzel Washington that said, "Ease is the greatest threat to progress than hardship."

4. Accept failure

> *"Success is not final, failure is not fatal: It is the courage to continue that counts."*
>
> – *WINSTON CHURCHILL*

I often hear a lot of successful people speak of failure as an antidote for where they are in life. In fact, Winston Churchill goes as far as saying "Success is the ability to go from failure to failure without losing your enthusiasm." The great thing about failure is that it introduces you to yourself, and helps you to learn at a rapid pace. In my stock market trading days, I made a lot of money, but

I also lost a lot of money and what kept me going after that was the fact that I looked at the money I had lost as tuition for the most expensive course. It was during this time that I learned a lot about managing my finances efficiently. I am happy to say that today my finances are in order and I am well on my way to financial freedom. Learn to fail forward, take every opportunity at failing because eventually, you will strike gold. Ultimately, remember that "Failure is a success if we learn from it." - Malcolm Forbes

5. Choose to be decisive

> *"Decisiveness is a characteristic of high-performing men and women. Almost any decision is better than no decision at all."*
>
> – BRIAN TRACEY

It can be argued that without making any decisions in life neither of us would progress in life. Life is full of all sorts of decisions from the moment you wake, up until you sleep. So making important decisions is crucial to our day-to-day activities. The ability to make decisions quickly and effectively will take you far. The more effective your decision-making process the easier it is for you to be productive in other areas of your life, it is for this reason that successful people like the late Steve Jobs wore the same outfit often, because of this understanding that the less time he spent deciding which outfit to wear, the potential to save on brainpower and time. Similarly, Mark Zuckerberg the founder of Facebook is often spotted in grey T-shirts and jeans. This is not to say that fashion and clothes are not important, but the point I am trying to drive home here is that these individuals understand that decision making is important and therefore do not want to make decisions about frivolous things such as what to wear or eat when they have other important decisions. The former president Barack

Obama is on the account saying that he wears grey and blue suits for this very reason. Obama further states that research has shown that "The simple act of making decisions degrades one's ability to make further decisions." Hence, the fewer decisions you have to make about things like what to wear or eat, the better – this has a special relationship with planning because failure to plan means more decision making at the last minute.

Silence is Golden: The Art of Silence

CHAPTER XI

"The lonely road to greatness is better than the crowded road to mediocrity."
– Matshona Dhliwayo.

The road to success can indeed be a lonely road, even the closest people won't always understand. That is to say, don't prematurely share your vision, it will cost you.

While there is this notion that success is a lonely road, I believe that this can be subjective. I say this because often, not everyone around you has the same vision, let alone the same drive and determination that you may possess. For this reason, it is essential to distinguish the fact that being lonely and choosing to be alone are two completely different things. You can choose to be alone because you need to focus and dedicate sufficient energy and time towards your goal. Therefore, while this may be a type of being alone, it is not entirely negative, in the end, it works out for the best.

Find the quiet moments in your life, for in them there is serenity. Your voice and mind are two of the most valuable assets you have at your disposal. To disregard their power is like living life as though you are dead because "Your inner voice is the voice of divinity." To hear it, "we need to be in solitude, even in crowded places."– A.R. Rahman

An ancient Egyptian proverb, "Silence is Golden," is perhaps one of the most prominent things ever said. When it comes to your vision and the ventures you want to pursue, you need to be careful how, when, and with whom you share this information. Contrary to popular belief, not everyone has your best interest at heart. People often celebrate your success with you until it overshadows theirs or gets to a level where they aspire to get to but haven't managed to achieve. Those with a lack of vision will often tell you that you cannot do things, simply because they have failed to accomplish anything of significance themselves. Often people will tell you that you can't do things because they have tried and failed at those things. That said, some people can only relate to your goals and vision based on their ability to comprehend. What I mean, is people who have never taken a leap of faith to pursue anything significant, will always relate to your ambitious goals from a cynical place.

That is why it is crucial to maintain the art of silence and only share it with those who will help you to fulfil the vision. Sharing too early will cause you a headache, you are likely to start hearing negative voices from people that may discourage your vision or goal.

In the Bible, the story of Joseph was that his father loved him more than any of his brothers. His father Jacob gifted him a coat of many colours which made his brothers envious when they saw it. He shared his dreams with his brothers on a few occasions, one dream, in particular, did not sit well with his older brothers. He shared that in this dream, all his brothers were kneeling to him, and he ruled over them. Following this, Joseph had another dream which he shared with the brothers saying, "I had another dream, and this time, the sun and moon and eleven stars were bowing down to me." When his brothers heard Joseph say this, they were unsettled, even his father rebuked him.

You can see from this example that some people's natural inclination is to want to see you do well, but just not better than them. If you know this story, you know that the brothers contemplated killing Joseph. But eventually sold him over to the Egyptians as a slave following a plea from one of Joseph's brothers Reuben not to kill him. He later goes through a process of trial and tribulation, even undergoing imprisonment, eventually becoming an Egyptian leader. We then learn, his brothers went through famine and their father Jacob sent them to Egypt to seek grain. We know that Joseph helped his brothers and forgave them for what they did to him many years before. (Genesis 37)

This is a prime example of how sharing your vision early, and with the wrong people could have implications. Joseph not only shared his dream once but twice, upon sharing for the first time, he would have noticed that the brothers didn't take the dream well. However, when he received the second dream, he still felt the need to share again. You see wisdom would have said, "I noticed that no one was happy when I shared this news last time, let me keep it to myself and let the dream manifest in its time." It is no surprise then that you may have experienced a negative response whenever you have shared your goals with others. Joseph felt free to share with his brothers, after all, they were family. Therefore, he didn't think twice about his safety, or anything potentially going wrong. The people closest to him were the ones who were part of his demise; well, at least at the time - these were the people closest to him.

It is essential to realize that anyone, including your relatives, family, and friends, could have the motive to discourage you from pursuing your dreams. Words live, so any negative word that is spoken to you, and anything you are involved in, could have a detrimental effect on your project or intended pursuit.

It's important to note, even your parents can discourage you; it is vital to share your goals and vision once you're sure. Better yet, once you have started pursuing your venture. On the other hand, some parents invest in their children early on. They understand that for their children to excel in life, they need as much support as they can get. Take, for example, popular golfer Tiger Woods, the Williams sisters who have dominated the tennis arena for years now. They understand something that others don't always get, and that is this, by investing in their children, they help them find their passions. This is a significant contributor to the success of their children. At only 15 years old, Andy Murray's parents sent him away to tennis school. Investing money with no return on investment guarantees, but this was for their son, and that's what mattered. Now, do you think that Andy Murray's parents will go without money for the rest of their lives? The answer is simply no. Their son is now successful, now it is time to enjoy the fruits of their sacrifices. Don't get me wrong, the point is not to invest in your children expecting to get something in return, but this sure does have its advantages. This is called paying it forward, giving your children the best possible opportunities to succeed will inadvertently benefit you in the long run. His parents are certainly not worried about a pension, because through their early sacrifices they are now able to reap the benefits.

It is okay to dream again, think like the child you once were when nothing in this world seemed to distract you and discourage you from pursuing your dreams. The attitude of a child is that if I can, I will, children dream without restrictions and aspire for greatness. What happens to some of us as we grow up, is that life beats us around; then we lose that zeal we once had in our youth. We take life too seriously and forget to dream, we forget to be playful, and we forget to smile. A rapper Sho Baraka once said a very profound quote that has stayed with me ever since, and it is that "You can be a dreamer but don't live in your bed." What this tells me is that while dreaming is a great and essential thing in life, the action is equally as crucial in making your dreams a reality. You need to engage your dreams through effort, take the first step.

Don't get me wrong, achieving your dream is no easy feat, then again, "Nothing worth having comes easy," - Theodore Roosevelt. The point being, when you have worked for your success, gone through sweat, blood, and tears. You are more likely to appreciate and enjoy your success as well as feel a sense of fulfilment and satisfaction. That is why I believe that success achieved from a place of total un-comfortability is much sweeter than the one gained from comfort. Stretching yourself beyond what you thought you were or are capable of is liberating and does an excellent deal for your mental capacity.

You must remember however that dreaming alone is not enough, a lot of people get stuck in what I call "Dreamland" and they never leave. "It does not do well to dwell on dreams and forget to live," said J.K Rowling. It is one thing to dream, but another to make that dream a reality. There are several definitions of what it is to dream, so for clarity, the kind of dreaming I am talking about is one which the Oxford dictionary defines as "a cherished aspiration, ambition, or ideal. Having a vision, conceptualising, and planning are all important ingredients to achieving success in your chosen field. However, doing that alone is not enough! There has to be an accompanying action to what you envision, after all, action speaks louder than words.

"Aspire to Inspire before you expire"

Aspiration is something you hope to achieve and to have hope is not a bad thing for where hope lies there are endless possibilities, only if you are willing to do what is necessary to achieve that which you desire. After all, hope keeps us going even when things get tough and life seems to get the better of us. Hope and faith go together, you can't have one and not the other if you are going to truly accomplish great feats in your life. The great book says, "Now faith is the substance of things hoped for, the evidence of things not seen." Hebrew 11:1

To have hope you must have faith, because how then do you build this tremendous courage to see things that are beyond your current situation. Aspiring is a good place to start, but once you have aspired, it is imperative to act on what you aspire for in the first place. A dream without a voice is just a dream, a dream without action is just mere imagination.

You are capable of achieving every desire and bringing goals to fruition no matter your circumstances. Learn to be grateful and live in anticipation as you put in the necessary work needed to achieve your goals. Denzel Washington says, "True desire in the heart for anything good is God's proof to you sent beforehand to indicate that it's yours already." So, exercise saying thank you in advance for the things you are hoping for.

When intentions go public

For many years I often wondered why it is that when I expressed my intentions about projects that I was working on, that they usually ended up stalling altogether. It took me a very long time to understand the principle behind not sharing ideas prematurely, but it cost me much in the process. You see, over the years, I have come to realize that action should be at the forefront of any productive person who considers themselves creative. I have come to understand that sharing ideas prematurely, while indicating the intention to pursue a project, can be very detrimental to your success. Believe in speaking things into the universe and having faith, but this must be done with utmost care and finesse. Only share your ideas with people who matter in the process of your success journey, people whom you know will contribute positively to your project. Others will find out once the project is a success.

A study titled 'when intentions go public' by Gollwitzer et al., found that the more you announce or express your intentions to others. Your mind automatically assumes you have accomplished the task. Your need for fulfilment is satisfied by sharing with other people. More so, I believe in the power of the words we speak as is made apparent in my earlier conversation on the I Am factor. It is fair to say that not everyone is your biggest fan. Therefore, you want to be careful that your idea does not land on the wrong ears, where someone can speak negatively about it. Leaving you to deal with the weight of negative words directed at your project. People by nature tend to be interested in what others are doing, so, limit what they talk about concerning you and your business by giving away a minimal amount of information. Ultimately, these are the same people that will laugh at you tomorrow should your plan not succeed, and guess what they'll remind you about your failure.

It can be said that we as humans feel accomplished when we share our intentions with our friends and loved ones. It makes us feel great for that moment, however, what we must now consider is whether sharing too soon is worth jeopardizing the success of your project. I think we can all agree that everyone wants to see their idea come to life and become a success. So then, where's the harm in keeping your intentions under wraps until everything is finalized and fully functional. Remember, that the same people you try to please today may turn against you tomorrow. Lecrae said that "if you live for their acceptance, you'll die from their rejection."

Be ready to share your plans with actions only, for it is the most significant expression of your intentions, show and tell rather than tell and show!

The benefits of Silence;

Some of the benefits of silence are detailed below, as a demonstration that silence is not only good regarding business but can help you to manage your life holistically also. When you exercise silence, you benefit from becoming;

Calmer and relaxed

Studies have shown that solitude has calming effects on your mind, and thus enhances your ability to overcome negative thinking and emotions.

Better intuition

Silence is an excellent way to build your gut instinct and intuition, two of the key drivers in making sound decisions. The more you have self-reflective talks with yourself, the more gut instinct you build.

Understanding yourself

Spending time with yourself away from all the noise and distractions will help you to gain a better understanding of who you are. Knowing yourself means that you can utilize your strengths and harness your energy in the right manner. "Knowing others is intelligence; knowing yourself is true wisdom. Mastering others is strength; mastering yourself is true power", Lao Tzu.

Discover your purpose

Silence helps you to discover who you are in the midst of all the commotion and chaos. The busyness of the day can be overwhelming, it is vital to switch off now and then. Gather your thoughts, this way, you can meditate and reflect on your purpose without interruptions.

Cure headaches and migraines

When you become silent, your breathing slows down, and your heart rate drops, and you get into this deep rest that allows you to cure any headaches and migraines.

There are plenty of other benefits that can be gained from silence apart from the obvious ones stated in this chapter. Start thinking about creating moments of calm in your life to create the ideal experience that you want. Remember, do not share your ideas prematurely, that will only create unnecessary pressure, and this will only work against you in the end.

Teach people how to treat you! Taking back control

"People will forget what you said, people will forget what you did, but people will never forget how you made them feel"

I expect excellent customer service, to be acknowledged and made to feel valued as a customer or client. How people treat you at their job is a good indication of their real-life character. In South Africa, there's a phrase 'Ubuntu' which means humanity, it doesn't matter whether you're at work or home. You should strive to leave a positive impression on people. It is often said that people won't remember you for what you did, but how you treated them. If you do something great for someone else, no matter how nice you treat them. If you mistreat them later, you will be remembered for the wrong treatment.

In my opinion, it is better to treat someone better than to shower them with meaningless gifts. Respect is a two-way street, it is always important not to let the actions of the other person change who you are. You do not have to stoop to someone's level just because they are nasty to you.

Proverbs 25-21 says, "If your enemy is hungry, give him food to eat; if he is thirsty, give him water to drink, In doing this, you will heap burning coals on his head, and the LORD will reward you."

I have been to shops where the attendant, although serving me, would carry on speaking to their colleague or seemed preoccupied with something else. Behaviours like this rub off me in the wrong way, I have often found myself debating whether, or not, I should leave such places. It is essential to know your worth as an individual, once you know this - you'll be aware of what's acceptable to you and what's not. Some of my mentors helped me shape how I respond to various situations by applying emotional intelligence. It does not mean you have to allow that behaviour in your presence, you have to teach people how to behave around you. For example, I have friends or people that I know who will not swear in my presence because they know I do not condone the language.

Similarly, whenever you receive bad customer service of any sort, you need not tolerate that sort of attitude. If you have to speak to a manager, please do it on the spot. First, give the perpetrator the chance to correct their mistake before you do this. If they refuse to acknowledge their error, then proceed to management. You could be helping them for a future occurrence, your intervention could be the help that the individual needs to become a better person in the future. Needless to say, their negative response will only perpetuate their undesirable attitude and for that reason, you should inform their manager about the issue to nip the attitude as soon as possible. Remember that what you embrace becomes your reality, only a change of thought and course can recreate a different reality - and one you're pleased with.

A lot of people go through life as characters and never the director and producer. They are playing to someone's script on life.

The art of 'Thank You': How appreciating the little things will make a big difference

For one reason or the other, it seems to me that a lot of people have lost the appetite to extend basic mannerisms when communicating and interacting with others. I personally find this behaviour appalling and hideous. As I said previously, teach people how to treat you. It is a trait of knowing who you are, what you will and won't tolerate. It is fair to say that, if you do not know what it is you stand for then, "You will fall for anything" – Alexander Hamilton.

Whenever I receive a text message from friends and family, and they have not bothered first to greet me. I often confront this behaviour because I find it rude and impersonal. A friend of mine once told me that I must go where I am celebrated and not where I am tolerated. When people appreciate you and treat you with respect, this will always go a long way.

I spent some of my younger years living with my grandmother Esther in Pretoria, South Africa, I had one of the best times of my life. However, one of my aunties whom I'll call Nandi for the purpose of this story was very abusive towards me verbally and would often utter derogative words at me, such as "Kwerekwere (Meaning foreigner)." This is because of my Zimbabwean heritage and where I came from. I remember once when my parents came over to visit as they'd usually do and I expressed my discomfort about being abused and my desire to leave. I left that very day and only visited my grandmother from then on, I decided enough was enough. My grandmother on the other hand had no idea why I suddenly decided to leave, I decided I did not want to burden her and strain her relationship with my aunty. You may wonder why my aunty did this if we are related, but the irony is that she didn't know that her mother was Zimbabwean, but had married a South African.

The moral of the story here is that through this experience I learned to control my emotions and to deal with the situation whether positive or negative in a mature manner. I understood then what it means when Maya Angelou said that "People will forget what you said, people will forget what you did, but people will never forget how you made them feel." This story with my aunt happened when I was less than ten years old, but I still remember it till this day. I am not a slave to my upbringing, but this is a reminder that you must never accept mediocrity, if the people around don't appreciate you then remove yourself.

It is good practice to make it clear what is and isn't acceptable. For example, I hate it when I receive a message, and there is no greeting. People will not know that what they are doing is not right by your standards, so you must let them know politely. This is important because, first of all, it shows respect, and secondly, it shows the person you are communicating with that you value them.

Never let people dictate to you how you should be treated, you have to set your boundaries. Those people that want to be around you, or let alone communicate with you need to do so in a respectful manner that upholds your dignity. Ensure that there is a balance to this and that you mutually respect the other person, and do not bring them to disrepute.

Let your name be synonymous with the word respect, it is not cowardice to say, 'Thank you, please, or let alone sorry when you know that you are wrong.' There is strength in displaying any of these traits, it should never be viewed as weakness. Whatever bad habits you have learned in the process can be unlearned, so do not write yourself off by thinking that you are incapable of doing these things.

The grass looks greener on the other side because they water it, the truth is - if you look after yours, and nurture it to fullness. Your grass will be as green as the grass on the other side.

The moral of the story, work at creating a better life, invest time and effort, and your grass will be evergreen.

> *"Work at creating a better life by investing time and effort into your life garden, and your grass will be evergreen."*

Freedom will unlock your greatness: Productivity without restrictions

The dictionary describes freedom as "The power or rights to act, speak, or think as one wants."

Sometimes, I found myself in situations that are restrictive and do not allow me the freedom of expression, as such, I only wanted to run away from such situations.

Case in point when I was younger as much as I respected my parents, I always liked to do things my way. Please understand when I say my way; I am not saying you have to disrespect your parents. I have a very independent mind when it comes to myself, an attitude I still possess.

Growing up in an African household, disciplining the children with a whip or belt or anything around was a standard way of living. At times you would even be asked to pick your punishment. For many years, as a child, I knew that whenever I or my younger brothers do something wrong, there were always consequences. As expected, we ignored the consequences in our young ignorant days and we paid for it in more ways than one.

I believe that with freedom comes a great deal of responsibility and should never be abused. I think that liberty is the start of responsibility and every individual deserves to be free. Whenever you place restrictive measures on someone who is supposed to be free by default, such an individual will find a way to escape you. You want to become a refuge for people and not a place where they feel they need to run away from.

I vividly remember at the age of 12 my dad saying "Ntoso, (as he affectionately calls me) I will not no longer discipline you by hand going forward, 'Usukhulile' - (Zulu for you are grown up now, you are a man)." He believed that I was capable of making sound decisions for my life.

That day although it may seem insignificant, it was a day whereby I assumed a lot of responsibility. It allowed me to see life from a different perspective, where I had to be responsible fast. One that encouraged me to keep positive friends around me. Often in my neighbourhood, I would find myself around guys older than me, but they enjoyed my company as much as I did theirs. As young as I was, I could hold an intellectual conversation with these grown men. I remember one of them (Nicolas) saying to me, "Have you noticed you are the only young star privileged to hang with us in this neighbourhood," I responded, "Yes I've noticed why is that?". Nicolas replied, "That's because you are mature and have a positive outlook on life."

I attributed a lot of the maturity to the freedom I have at home and being allowed my individuality. Have you ever wondered why most people who are told not to do something always end up doing it? Well, my dad once simply put it this way "Once someone is told not to do something in a restrictive way, they'll be curious to explore."

Freedom is fundamental in life - have you ever noticed that often your desire of buying a particular item vanishes, once you have enough money. Whereas, before you have enough money, you desire it so much? I find it interesting that most of the time we fantasize about something only to lose interest once we have the resources. What this tells me is that somehow, we always want things we can't afford. But once we have enough disposable income, our thoughts become much more objective and calculative. Suddenly, you can distinguish between necessities and non-important things. Again, this is the freedom that finances bring, the ability to think freely and objectively.

Why do people do the opposite of what they're told? Reverse psychology.

There is another side of the coin to this theory; however, some people simply do not think smart once they have the money they longed for. Not everyone is smart enough to understand the importance of freedom, some struggle even after obtaining freedom. They tend to go back to their former state after a short while. Growing up in South Africa, I had a neighbour who used to work for an affluent car dealer in the city of Johannesburg. He would go throughout the week saying he needed money to buy necessities for his family. However, every Friday was payday for him. Everyone in the neighbourhood would know that he had been paid, it was all in his step and sudden boastful behaviour, how could one miss it. He showered his friends with alcohol and food through the weekend. As soon as Sunday came, he'd be back to square one asking to borrow money for transport from the very people he was showing off to.

The same can be true for financial freedom if you are willing to embrace delayed gratification, be ready to reap great rewards. Often, people are comfortable with the idea of knowing they've got a guaranteed salary at the end of the month. It is one thing to have a job and still pursue your goals than to have a job and forget all about the thing that makes you tick.

I have often heard the saying that those that do not chase and aim for their dreams and ambitions will be hired by those who do. It is quite simple, those who can predict the future can charge a premium for it, and those that can't forecast will have to pay the premium. Someone once said that some people think that a business that takes 3 years to become profitable took a long time. However, they do not feel that 10 to 40 years working for someone is a long time to be broke.

There is power in individuality: Our power is what sets us apart.

CHAPTER XIV

"There's a thin line between being inspired, and being a carbon copy of someone else".

I grew up in South Africa in my early years up until I was 16 years old. I always felt like an outcast and I never really fitted into my surroundings, I was never like any of my peers and for many years I felt inadequate. I knew deep down that I was meant for greater things, but it would be nice to fit in at the same time. I remember hanging out with one of the older guys in my neighbourhood and he told me something that has stuck with me since. He said, "Dave we hang with you because you are mature and none of your peers have the same calibre of character that you do", it was at this moment that I realised that I was made for greater things and that my life was not heading for mediocrity. I learned that my individuality was not a curse but a blessing in disguise, I began to embrace what sets me apart, and only then was I able to channel my energy into my purpose.

I have come to understand that the more you ignore yours' and other people's individuality and traits, you will only get frustrated. Individuality is what colours our environment and brings vibrancy to our world.

Sho Baraka, a rapper once said, "Everyone sounds the same in music nowadays" he raps that everyone sounds like Drake the rapper, in his words "If I wanted to listen to Drake, I would just listen to Drake." A massive indication that some people have lost their identity and uniqueness in the process of trying to emulate others. I believe it is great to learn from other people and be inspired by their success to be the better version of yourself. However, I do not agree with measuring your progress against other people. Just because someone lives their life a certain way, does not mean that you start copying everything they do. So much that if you haven't got a new car or a modern sofa they've got, you become bitter and don't feel accomplished. There's a thin line between being inspired, and being a carbon copy of someone else.

For couples, comparing your spouse to someone else's other half is a grave mistake. You have to appreciate what you have and cultivate it, remember that people only let you see what they want you to see. When they fight and argue, they don't post that on social media, and just because it looks appealing, you don't know what's behind the closed doors. Equally, what works for someone else won't work for you, find your rhythm and pace in life. Be careful, you don't alienate the people that are closest to you by trying to force them into a lifestyle that they don't feel comfortable with. This will cause them to drift further away from you and eventually, they'll have no choice but to leave if it means they can't be themselves around you.

Acknowledge your scars: Wear them as a badge of honour

CHAPTER XV

"The best people all have some kind of scar."
- Kiera Cass

Scars are there to show you that you are a survivor. Scars will remind you of the event you survived, tell you the time and place but can't keep you there. It is now a memory, nonetheless a necessary reminder of where you are coming from, and the obstacles you've had to overcome. Rick Warren put it this way "I am a product of my past, but I'm not a prisoner of my past."

History teaches us about ourselves and where we come from, but it cannot predict our future, we carve out our future by what we do today. Only our present can influence our future, it is a ripple effect. Take, for example, someone who is health-conscious and eats well or exercises, against someone who pays no regard to the same. The person who exercises regularly will inevitably reap great rewards health-wise. The individual that fails to look after his or her health today has an opportunity to change this tomorrow as long they are still able, alive, and willing. So ultimately, even the mistakes done today are not permanent if one is willing to work towards a different outcome tomorrow. There is always a second chance, but the right attitude is required to capitalize on it.

Always have the present and future in your mind. Imagine running a marathon and pacing yourself for the kilometres ahead, but as you set off, you are tempted to keep looking back to see what is behind you. If you have ever been involved in a race, then you will know that looking back as you are running consumes a great deal of energy. First of all, you lose focus of where you are going, this, in turn, puts you in danger of potentially tripping, and when you trip there is a possibility of injury. It is advisable to use this energy to charge forward. I am yet to see Olympians like Usain Bolt, or Mo Farah looking back while running - they focus on the race ahead and give it their best. This way, they are not intimidated nor distracted unnecessarily along the way. Focus is significant to one's journey if you are going to accomplish greatness.

Do not live in the past, keep moving forward because today is a new day, yesterday is a memory and tomorrow is the future. Don't get me wrong, you can look back to see how far you have come, it is not entirely a bad thing. Just don't spend too much time looking back, since this consumes a great deal of energy and won't do you any good in the long run. Looking back means you are not looking towards where you are going, and like I said this can lead to a crash or catastrophic event. I remember scaling up the Peak District Mountain sometime in the summer of 2018, I had never climbed a mountain so high in my life, as I went up further and further. I remember taking a peek behind to see how far I had come, and I was so high up that looking back gave me goosebumps and butterflies in my stomach. Suddenly, the fact that I was so high up gave me a slight fright, whereas I was okay before looking back.

Pay careful attention to what it is you are looking back at, and ask yourself, is it necessary? Will it motivate you to keep going or deter you? If your answer is "no" then do whatever will produce the opposite result.

Just as scars show your resilience, isn't it interesting that sometimes the food that has the most nutrients for the body does not always taste as lovely as you want it to? But you eat or consume them nonetheless because of the health benefits and implications they yield or provide for the body.

Equally, life's most vital and crucial lessons are sometimes hard to embrace. We must continue to learn from our mistakes to grow and move forward. Going to the gym often requires a strong will and discipline, one must be willing to endure physical pain for a particular outcome. You will have heard the phrase no pain, no gain, now I've often wondered why the things that propel us or prepare us for greatness have to be painful. The reason is, to get rid of old habits and behaviours. You will have to go through a process of refining, to get rid of that stubborn fat, or improving your time management. It can also improve your social relations with friends and family - it takes tenacity to change poor habits to good ones.

People often say the truth hurts, and that is because the denial of the truth can only keep you in fear. The truth will help you grow, and positive criticism is worth its weight in gold; however, the truth given with an agenda of divisiveness is not worth it. Truth can build you up, the fact will help you to develop yourself into a better person. Speaking the truth gives you a clear conscience and allows you to live a worry-free life.

Space rocket sheds off weight on the way up because it can't reach great heights without that. The space rocket is a very intricate and yet beautifully assembled piece. It is made up of two to three different rockets stuck together to form one giant rocket – this is called the stages. When the rocket sets off into space, lower stages begin to break away from the main rocket. As their fuel gets used up, only the top rocket makes it to its destination. In like manner, in life, some people, and processes are only but for a season. Clinging to those things or people can only drag you down. It is time to elevate, you must realize that to go higher you must remove any and everything that takes away from your energy unnecessarily.

The power of repetition & Affirmation: Using your words to shape your future

CHAPTER XVI

"The best thing I ever heard said about me, is what I said to myself."

Repeating something over and over will yield results, whether positive or negative.

It has been said that the law of attraction can be used for everyday living. However, to exercise this effectively and produce results, there lies a critical ingredient that most people overlook. This ingredient is simply called repetition.

In my daily life, I have often struggled to break out of habits as most of us do. However, I found that confronting these failures and acknowledging them allows you to think about solutions. A positive outlook will always take you far, and how you approach each situation determines the outcome. Let's think about the former President of the United States of America. During his senator days, Barrack Obama's campaign mantra was "Yes We Can." People had long been seeking something new, something that would reignite their passion and hope for the country. People said "Yes we can" so much so that anything contrary didn't make sense. People gravitated towards a belief based on doing the impossible and ushering in a new wave of politics. President Obama won the race against John McCain of the Republicans' in 2008, he later got re-elected for another term in 2013.

In life, I've come to realize that attempting something is far much better than not trying. It is a grave mistake to think about failure when you think of attempting anything because you automatically set yourself up for failure. It is, however, wise to think about actions that will help you make calculated decisions on how to execute the task at hand or that business venture you're thinking about starting.

Words shape your environment, and using the right words is not always easy. However, they are crucial to your future and environment. As humans, it is easy to become an insecure individual that lacks confidence and says things filled with fear to connote little or no self-esteem. It is crucial, however, to ensure that negative thoughts are kept captive, out of sight (at least in theory), and kicked to the curb. Maximize your capacity to think positively, and part of doing this is ensuring that you have the right people around you, guard your space. Speak confidently about yourself, do not look for this from other people. Be your best cheerleader and encourager. Les Brown said something along the lines of "The best thing I ever heard said about me, is what I said to myself." It is clear to see why a lot of successful people believe in speaking things into existence and then waiting for them to become a reality. Once you put out the word into the universe, everything that lives in the world of the said 'word' starts looking for you. Mohammed Ali said, "I am the greatest, I said that before I even knew, I was." In another instance, famous comic actor Jim Carrey once wrote himself a cheque for $10 million in 1985 and had it dated 10 years in the future. In 1995 during the Thanksgiving season, he found out he had been offered a starring role in the film Dumb and Dumber for $10 million. What am I trying to say? What matters the most is what you say about yourself not what other people say about you. If you can imagine it, if you can dream it, if you can fathom it – surely it is yours. All you have to do is work hard, and be diligent in whatever it is you are doing. And everything will come full circle to meet you at your point of need.

There are certain people in my life (including friends and family) that I have learned to never regard anything they say or do, because of their inability to deliver. It has become just plain words, I set my expectations low, and that way, nothing catches me off guard, and often I am right. There are certain people I have to invite to essential events in advance knowing that they'll turn up at least almost on time.

Rest assured that having this type of attitude is not the end of the world, as you can always do something about this – if this is a bad habit that you have developed over time, guess what? You can unlearn it just as you have learned it over time. Taking your power back starts with recognizing that you need help. Secondly, following up on the recommendations and areas of improvement require practical day-to-day steps such as aiming to be extra early for meetings by at least 20-30 minutes. Practice keeping your word by starting with minuscule things, and one step at a time, you will become better at mastering this skill.

Affirmation you can apply to your life

- My future reflects what I envision now.

- I am successful in all my endeavors.
- I am healthy and of a sound mind.
- I am more than a conqueror, and nothing will derail me.
- I have endless talents that I will begin to use today.
- I am wealthy and successful.
- I believe in myself, I am motivated and dedicated.
- I am fearless and confident.
- I am a leader with world-class resilience.
- I am in command of my life.
- I am superior to negative thoughts and low energy.
- I am success personified.

You can add to this list in line with what you want to see manifest in your life. Write down several affirmations and refer to them daily, and as time goes on this will start to feel attainable and from then on, it's only a matter of time until what you say turn to reality. The aim is to maintain consistency in this area and you will start to see your surroundings change for the better.

Learn to choose your battles wisely: Just because there's a war doesn't mean you have to engage.

"When a demand is placed on you, you will rise to the occasion."

CHAPTER XVII

You might have heard the phrase, "There are many ways to skin a cat" - Seba Smith. But I believe that finding the right cat to 'skin' is equally as important. You must choose your battles carefully and prudently, and if there no spoils to be won in a war, the best course of action is not to engage. Reserve your energy, for there will come a day when a demand is placed on you that requires your strength. Sir Winston S. Churchill said that "You will never reach your destination if you stop and throw stones at every dog that barks.".

Similarly, my late aunt (My dad's sister) once told me that "As long as I am alive I will never be able to stop birds from flying over my head." This stuck with me since and over the years I learned to distance myself from negative people whose intention was always to get into any and every argument. In my secondary school days, although I was quite laid back, it was a well-known thing that I was not to be provoked. I attended the same school as my two younger brothers and often I would be caught up in their troubles trying to protect them. I remember one of the students wanted to fight me as I tried to defend my younger brother and I had to ask myself whether it was worth it. It was that day that I decided not to engage in any fights, instead, I avoided anything that would draw me to that world. There was absolutely nothing to be gained I promised myself to never fight again and I have remained that way since. Equally, in your daily life, it is important to ensure there are no unnecessary distractions. Tackle worthy wars in your everyday life, you don't have to pay attention to everything that prods at you. There are plenty of instances when you'll find yourself challenged, and you will have a choice to make. Do I engage in this challenge or let it go? Is it worth my time, and if so, what gain is it going to bring my way? Now when I say to gain, I'm not necessarily talking about tangible increases such as money or resources only. NO! Your benefit could be intangible. For example, you might be interested in learning about how a business is been operated because you have no prior experience. You may know someone or a start-up business that you feel would be useful in your learning journey. What you may do is offer to volunteer and learn the business processes to enhance your business insight and experience. While you may not receive any payment for this type of work, you will be able to gain invaluable experience. On the other hand, you could evaluate whether this way is best, and if not, enrolling in a professional course may be the way forward. All this will depend on your capacity and what you can afford, and this can be broken down into the following time, cost, or quality implications. It may be that practical experience is much more valuable than attending a classroom course. This is where your evaluation comes in, you must be honest and realistic with yourself. There are no one shoe fits all, you have to be clear and strategic about what you want to do and what is involved in each decision you make.

In the year 2017, I made one of the most challenging decisions of my life, I went back to university. A place I'd vowed never to set foot again following my undergraduate degree. I thought this way because I had worked in various sectors for several years, from customer service to my last job as a building manager. I started to re-evaluate my life and where I wanted to be compared to where I was, and the answer was simple I wasn't happy. I looked at the challenge before me and weighed it out against my situation. I was in a comfortable job, I concluded that my salary did not match up to the lifestyle I wanted to live. Admittedly, I had to do something about this, it was at this point that I applied to Nottingham Trent University. This was beyond money needs, I also needed a place where I could make a positive contribution through strategic decisions. Weeks later I was offered admission for a master's degree program in quantity surveying. Even so, I was still very much anxious and almost considered doing building surveying instead as I thought it would be an easier option. Quantity Surveying was a course that I had no prior knowledge about, whereas building surveying would've been an easy escape. The fascinating thing about quantity surveying is that it comprises of everything I considered myself not good at. My strengths and weaknesses had to be weighed out, I had never considered mathematics as my strong point, as well as when it came to drawing, I never did finish secondary education, I left South Africa three years before I was supposed to graduate. This meant I only had a basic understanding of my subjects at the time. As you may guess the course involved both elements amongst others. I was entirely out of my depth and comfort zone here. There I was during the first week thinking, "what did I just get myself into doing this

113

course?" I couldn't understand a single word of the technical jargon that was being used.

In due course, I began to find my way around and started to grasp the lectures slowly. Believe it or not, I performed better studying my MSc than I ever did on my undergrad degree. This, for me, became a great lesson in the ever cliché saying that "Whatever you put your mind to, you can do it." This reaffirmed the words by Confucius for me that say, "He who thinks he can, and he who thinks he can't are both right."

The MSc was not easy to do by the slightest, I was challenged in every direction. I remember during the first week, I almost quit, thinking, "I can't do this; it is very complicated." However, I stuck through it and persevered throughout the turbulence of workload and learning new concepts. Before the end of the course, I had managed to secure a role with Highways England. A reputable organization in which I worked in the commercial department, and had plenty of opportunities to make strategic decisions. All this because I dared to stretch myself and increase my mental capacity. My career progression has only gotten better and better since I now make executive decisions and manage some staff with my role with a local council.

The truth of the matter is that each milestone in life will stretch you and increase your capacity. It is crucial to put yourself in the most uncomfortable situations and places as often as you can. Do this as much as possible, and you will grow, this is where you develop your ability to withstand everything that is thrown at you. Ultimately, "If you are only willing to do what's easy, life will be hard. But if you are willing to do what's hard, life will be easy." - T. Harv Eker

In my last job, I was a building manager, and part of my role involved dealing with day-to-day operations. Before this, I had no real management experience except for theoretical approaches.

Initially, when I applied for this role, I thought, "well let me try my luck," but I knew for sure I had no prior experience in this type of work. I had a vague understanding of the role and what was involved. I applied regardless and succeeded in getting the role, and immediately in my first week, I was thrown in the deep end because the person responsible for conducting my induction was off sick for what turned out to be a whole month. Immediately I found myself in a situation where I had to take charge and go through a baptism of fire. I had to learn a lot of processes by myself with very minimal guidance. My willingness to learn and conquer this new role kept me steadfast and allowed me to learn quickly. The moral of the story is that you can never be fully ready for what's to come, something is bound to take you by surprise one way or the other, the only thing that will keep you in those scenarios is strong character and willingness.

It is clear to me that no one is born with the knowledge of their full potential, but through discovery and a sense of curiosity, we then find these things out. And a lot of this has to do with creating opportunities in your life to never stay the same. Be curious, be inquisitive, seek, and eventually, you'll find. I dare say no one has ever gained an insight into their full potential through sitting it out and waiting for it to come to them, or through comfort. You need to stretch yourself and allow growth to happen.

When a demand is placed on you, you will rise to the occasion.

The pain and struggle you encounter when you begin any task or journey in life can utterly demoralize you from attempting to go further or take a second step. Once you're faced with pain, the thought of moving forward, knowing you'll encounter more pain makes the task daunting.

As an avid gym-goer, I often have to fight against a lot of thoughts within my head. One time, I was training chest, and as I continued doing my sets on the bench press. I started to struggle to bench 60kgs, and the thought of doing something heavier was unfathomable given my struggle with the present reps. I knew I had to increase my weight on my next set because I was following a prescribed program. My brain kept saying, "That last set you did was your maximum." I remember thinking "surely even if I did 1 more rep that would be sufficient for the100 kgs. Guess what! I did 4 reps on the first set and 5 reps on the second set of 100kgs. The moral of the story is that you always have more in you, never look at your circumstances and allow them to circumvent your destiny. In whatever you do never settle, Les Brown talks about the fact that a lot of people have settled in life, whether it's settling for a relationship they shouldn't be in, a job they hate, friendships that are going nowhere, the list goes on. Brown further likens this type of settling to that of an individual making an out-of-court settlement, for whatever reason just like this type of settlement a lot of people are taking less than they deserve, or what they intended to receive. Often that is because they believe that they will not receive it.

I have learned that challenges will force your back against the wall. I understand that certain situations can force us to settle, but my point here is that it is crucial to make sure that you remember your worth even during the storm. When all else has failed and it seems like you have no choice, never sell yourself short.

Your Obstacles Are A Stepping Stone To Greatness

CHAPTER XVIII

"Obstacles are things a person sees when he takes his eyes off his goal."
— E. Joseph Cossman

Your highest potential is unleashed when you defy the obstacles that would set you back under normal circumstances.

Being backed against a corner will make you engage your inner idealist. It will propel you to your most important purpose. While comfortability allows you to sit back on your potential, pressure does the opposite. A late pastor of mine Jason Steele once said that people often want olive oil, but they do not appreciate the process that olives have to go under. They have to be pressed, and a lot of pressure applied to them, and the result becomes what we consume and enjoy in our daily lives. By the same token, if you think about gold, it undergoes a melting process under extreme heat, 1064 degrees Celsius to be precise. What comes out at the end; however, is something of sheer beauty, a jewel that holds a lot of value regardless of the various environments it would have had to endure and go through. Most people know that gold is scarce, you have to dig underground to find it. It is often covered by soil and is usually found deep into the earth. In light of this, it is evident that despite any challenges you face, you are on a journey that cannot be determined by your short-term circumstances. You shouldn't judge your present based on how things look momentarily. To overcome, you will need to envision how you want your life to look each day. Incorporate a visual representation of how you see your future, create a vision board, and fill it up with everything you want to achieve.

I remember back in South Africa as a young lad growing up, I was in my early teens, and for some reason. I kept picturing myself in a place other than the one I was in. I knew that there had to be something better. Don't get me wrong, my early years in South Africa were awesome till we moved to the township. I began to experience life from a different perspective. The things I once took for granted, like living in central Johannesburg and having access to excellent facilities and amenities, swimming pools seemed like a thing of the past in this new place. Nonetheless, my positive thinking kept me going, knowing that whatever I put my mind to, I can achieve.

Individuals that have achieved great feats in life are those that have defied a lot of odds. Yes, they have faced challenges, but it's how they overcome them that sets them apart from the rest.

I remember delivering a speech once about individuals who have challenged the status quo despite the various challenges placed before them. I spoke of a young lady whom I'd met in London the weekend before the speech. This young lady's name is Victoria, I vividly remember getting off the train at London St Pancras station. I took the escalators down and proceeded to walk towards the exit and halfway through I heard a well-played piano to the tune of Isn't She Lovely by Stevie Wonder. An angelic voice sang beautifully to the keyboard. I started walking in the direction of the piano. As I got closer, it sounded more inviting. Coming from a musical background myself, I was impressed to hear such excellence on the keyboard.

I approached the piano and just stood there in awe as I took in the beautiful vibrations and ambience this young lady created through her playing and singing. It was apparent that this was a talented and passionate individual by how she played and exhumed confidence. Once she was done playing, I immediately went over to introduce myself, "Hello, you play and sing so beautifully" I echoed, and Victoria smiled and said, "Thank you very much" as she carried on playing some more. I asked, "Do you mind if I film you play?" and she replied, "Sure, that's absolutely fine."

I noticed something about Victoria as she continued to play the piano, her right arm was amputated. Despite this her skill on the piano was impeccable. Maybe Victoria has questioned whether or not she is good enough given her circumstances in past. Regardless, Victoria has risen above the odds and challenged the status quo. When the going got tough, she did not check out and disqualify herself, instead, she found other ways to do the same thing. Just because one door closes, does not mean you check out, there are many other alternatives and options. Thomas A. Edison, the inventor of the light bulb, failed many times before he eventually found a solution that would revolutionize the way we light our homes and establishments. He said, "I did not fail, I just found ten thousand ways that won't work."

I went over to talk to Victoria after she played for the second time, "Hey, you play and sing amazingly," I said. "Thank you, I'm glad to hear you enjoyed it," she replied. Victoria's talent drew me to her, I could see the passion that oozed out of her as she played and sang so beautifully. I want you to understand that a person's shortcomings and or disadvantages are not the determining factor on what is produced as an output, instead, it is the beginning of discovery. Once you know your weaknesses, you can work on improving for the better, you can find alternatives around doing the same task albeit more creatively. Nick Santonastasso who is one of the four people with a rare genetic condition Hanhart syndrome, which means he is missing both legs and one arm once said that "The truth is that there are no excuses, and the biggest disability is a bad mindset." Despite this Nick has managed to become an influential and inspiring bodybuilder with a build that some can only dream of, he is a well-known public speaker who has shared stages with the likes of Tony Robbins and continues to inspire millions around the world.

I remember reading an article about disabled people that spoke about stereotypes. The consensus was that disabled people do not want people to feel sorry for them. Instead, they want people to treat them with respect and equality.

I remember watching a Black Coffee interview, an internationally acclaimed DJ from South Africa whose real name is Nkosinathi Maphumulo, or Nathi for short. He spoke about a car accident that left him with a paralyzed arm. While the nation of South Africa was celebrating the release of Nelson Mandela from prison on the 11th of February 1990. A car driver ploughed into the crowd leaving two people dead and others injured including Black Coffee who was immediately rushed to the hospital to seek medical help. He was battling scars from the accident, as a result, was diagnosed with a brachial plexus injury. The medical dictionary describes it as "a group of nerves that originate in the spinal cord in the neck and travel down the arm." These muscles control the shoulder, elbow, wrist, and hand, while also providing tactile sensations.

It seemed that everything had turned against Black Coffee at this very moment and that his dreams and aspirations of becoming a DJ had been shattered by that unfortunate accident. Despite all of this, Black Coffee did not fold in the face of adversity, I can imagine there were days where he pondered to himself and thought "why me?" These moments of questioning yourself and doubting will occur to most of us at one point or another. However, the most important thing to do is not to dwell on those moments but to press on. We would be best placed to hold those thoughts and tell them, "You will not hold me captive", and when life has thrown all its challenges at you do not cave in and give up.

Black Coffee did not let the accident deter him from following his dreams, instead, he worked harder at mastering his skills with just one arm and today he travels all over the world playing the most coveted stages. His circumstance only forced him to find other ways of creativity. Never make an excuse about not being able to do something the way you planned to, or with the method you wanted to use. Rather erase that from your mind and find a thousand other alternatives. See those impossibilities as opportunities, see those barriers as steppingstones. Black Coffee wrote on his Facebook account once and said, "I used to hate this day...every year it would depress me. But I've come a long way since then, and I've learned so much about myself. Now I celebrate this day because it changed my life. Because on this day, I learned to push all the limits, and I've worked twice as hard to realize my dreams in music. And today 26 years later I'm shooting a cover for ELLE magazine". He described faith as the driving force behind how he achieved his dreams. Black Coffee's album Pieces of Me achieved platinum status less than a month after it was released. He has since collaborated with artists such as Drake, Alicia Keys,

David Guetta, and more to date. In Black Coffee's words during an interview with djmag he said "If you were to ask me, do you wish it never happened? I would say no. It came with so much." A prime example of never limiting yourself, you are a powerful being beyond measure.

I am convinced that the hard and challenging times in our lives are the necessity that chisels and sculptures our characters. It is in these moments that we find out what we are truly capable of, people discover their capabilities when faced with what seemingly looks like a dead end.

I was browsing my Instagram account one day when I came across an inspirational bodybuilder Steve Alexie who has cerebral palsy. He trains as hard as the next man, and shows no signs of being a victim, he has competed in numerous bodybuilding competitions. He has shown time and time again that his health condition is only but that, it does not mean that he should give up and quit - he has found the light where others might have seen gloom. He has refused to let his life be determined by cerebral palsy. The point is every individual no matter the race, colour, background, financial standing, or family history has the potential to be the best they can be. If only you believe, then the rest will follow. It won't be easy, it will require persistence, hard work, drive and determination, the ability to laugh in the face of adversity.

An alternative way of doing something makes you a genius and not a weirdo. It is time for society to see people that have risen beyond their obstacles as heroes. They have figured out their purpose, while many still are lost trying to figure out what it is they are here on earth for. In life you will face challenges, it is inevitable. It is what you do when you are backed against the wall that matters, when one possibility closes, many others are waiting to be unlocked.

Pay Attention to the noise around & listen to your gut instinct

"Sometimes you have to believe in someone else's belief in you until your belief kicks in."
- Les Brown

People will hint at your strengths and weaknesses, listen to those little voices. The best way to find out what you are good at will often come from those telling you that you are brilliant at something. For so long, I was tirelessly trying to figure out what it was I was good at. All the while, my friends, family, and colleagues always alluded to the fact that am I good at giving sound advice and keeping my poise under pressure. In addition, they would point to the fact that I am good when speaking. I overlooked all of this and continued to pursue other things I felt that I was good at. I went from owning a small clothing label to printing clothes, starting a community interest company, and pursuing a music career. All of these things kept me busy, but I worked tirelessly at them and never did become excellent at any of them. After all, it was the effort that counted at this stage, and I needed to keep busy. Being creative is sometimes a gift and a curse because you try and do everything because you can, as a result never master any. This is until you give one thing your undivided attention.

It took the rejection of my sock business idea for me to finally pay attention to what it is I am really good at. I joined a university program for entrepreneurs (The Hive) at Nottingham Trent University. I remember pitching my idea with enthusiasm and vigour, only to be told by my advisor that he thought the idea wouldn't work in practice. I was disappointed, here I was before this person who was supposed to help me, but instead, he told me that my idea was not viable. He advised me to stay on the program and that I might eventually come up with another plan. As disappointed as I was, I decided to stay and continue seeking help and advice. It was after a few weeks that it finally dawned on me that I had been staring at my gift in the face this whole time and didn't realize it right in front of me. I am a great problem solver, excellent at giving advice, a great speaker, with a brilliant business mind. I had a level 4 public speaking qualification from the English-Speaking Board. It was at this point that my company Inspire Speaking was born. Indeed, it is true that "Sometimes you have to believe in someone else's belief in you until your belief kicks in." - Les Brown

The truth is that your value does not depreciate because you are facing challenges and life has kicked you around and slapped you a bit. Imagine a £10 note, you can do anything to this note, put it in water, step on it and tear it. It never loses its value, someone can tape it together and still buy something with it, or take it to the bank to be exchanged. When you face challenges in life see yourself as the £10 note that withstands all adversities and can still come out strong on the other side.

It is important to listen to what people are saying around you and about you. However, be mindful that not every voice is worth listening to, I suggest you learn to pick out the good and leave out the not-so-good from every situation you find yourself. Listen to the voice of reason within you, or as some would call it, "your conscience", it is a potent tool when used to its full potential.

Often, I am hard on myself, I ignore the voice of reason that says, "Do it this way" or "it's time to stop and try another time." The majority of the time when I didn't listen to this voice, the aftermath was devastating. Why did I not listen to that voice of reason that said, "Stop trading the stock market today, take the profit and start again tomorrow." What was a great productive day, would quickly turn into a loss in my early days of trading the stock market. Lack of self-control is a dangerous trait, one should take calculated measures to ensure deliberate control is exercised at all times.

I often found myself going back to the market, lo and behold, I let my emotions get the better of me. And eventually lost all my capital in one day. All the two thousand six hundred pounds I had in my account.

Instinct is often neglected and shoved away and even suppressed at times. If we only listened to this mighty thing called the voice of reason, or conscience. A lot of things would make sense, and we would save ourselves such a big headache and possible heartache in a lot of things. The voice of reason is simply that calm voice in the background that helps us make those crucial decisions. It helps us to see the bigger picture in many ways other than one.

What's age got to do with it?

CHAPTER XX

"Anyone who stops learning is old, whether at twenty or eighty. Anyone who keeps learning stays young,"
- Henry Ford.

One of the biggest mistakes one can make is to think that their success or lack thereof is dependent upon their age. Believe me when I say that age has nothing to do with it. I often hear a lot of people say the words "I haven't got enough time," or "I am old now, my time has passed." These people have checked out of life, they seem to think that somehow their age determines where they are, or where they'll end up. It is a grave mistake to believe that age is the critical driver in determining your success as you pursue your dreams.

Let's revisit the word dream, according to dictionary.com, a dream is "A cherished aspiration, ambition, or idea."

What this is telling me is that ultimately, you are responsible for your life. You first must envision your desired future, aspire to achieve it through dedication, ambition, and hard work. It is okay to have a desired future but make no mistake this is going to require your blood, sweat, and tears. Those around you will help where possible if you have the right bunch, but ultimately the responsibility of making your dreams come true stays solely with you. Remember that age and size are numbers. It's the attitude you bring to clothes that make the difference" - Donna Karan. Perspective is so critical to everything that you do, Zig Ziglar said: "It is your attitude, more than your aptitude that will determine your altitude." Next time you are confronted by those negative thoughts of inadequacy that say, "You are not good enough." Look in the mirror, and say; "I am a conqueror, I am a winner, I deserve everything good that is coming my way, I am wealthy beyond measure, and my dreams are valid, and I am a magnet for wealth." Observe how your mentality suddenly changes the more you repeat these phrases to yourself. You will notice how you will start believing that your dreams are achievable because it is. If you can believe it, then you can achieve it.

Interestingly, when most of us were growing up, we yearned to be adults. Yet, now that we are adults, we find it complimentary to be told that we look young and wish to relive our younger years again. The truth is you must embrace your present, this is where you stand today. Do not wish your life away by living the life that is neither here nor there, do not look at the past and wish it was here, but rather live in the present and embrace every moment of it. Make no mistake, a bit of reflection is not a problem for how do you know where you are going if you do not see how far you have come? Just don't dwell on it too long, look forward, and press on because today needs your undivided attention if you are going to see results. I often tell my father during our heart-to-heart conversations that he can do anything he wants to do if he commits to it. Once my father said, "My son, where I grew up, we had no internet or good education, so there's a limit to how far I can go in life." I told him that "You can re-educate yourself and learn something new because where you come from does not determine your future." The truth is a lot of people associate their upbringing with how far in life they can go, where they can work, and how much they can achieve. This is not true; it all starts with a desire to want to change and be better. Although, you are a product of your past, remember that you are not a prisoner of your past as Rick Warren put it.

A lot of people may know about the Kentucky Fried Chicken (KFC) brand, but what most people don't know is how it came to be. Colonel Sanders, as he was affectionately known, is the founder of KFC, and his childhood and adult life tell the story of a brave soul and relentless individual. At just six years of age, his father passed away, and Colonel had to assume responsibility for his two siblings, taking up the role of cooking. In his early years, he had already worked in many jobs such as insurance salesman, railroad fireman amongst others. Around the age of forty, Colonel began selling his chicken through his service station and would later go on to close the restaurant in 1952. At the age of sixty-five Colonel Sanders retired, he felt like a failure at this stage, so much so he even considered suicide. On his first day of retirement, he received a cheque from the government for the sum of $105. It was at this point, that instead of writing his will, he thought about ideas, and how good of a cook he was. He borrowed $87 and went door to door selling his chicken using his special recipe.

Today, we enjoy KFC because Colonel did not give up on his dream. KFC is a big franchise organization today, selling amazing chicken made from his special recipe according to verge.com and biography.com.

In the words of Colonel Harland Sanders, "There's no reason to be the richest man in the cemetery. You can't do any business from there".

There's also Fred De Luca, the late Subway owner who co-founded Subway at the age of 17 years old. He started the business with funds received from a family friend Peter Buck who borrowed Fred $1000. The first store failed, but Fred did not get deterred. Instead, he started another one, and this time within a decade, he had around 32 stores through the franchise model. Today subway is in over 40 locations worldwide and has a revenue of 10.8 billion-plus in sales each year.

The lesson here is that age has absolutely no bearings on how your future pans out. You can become anything you want to be; you can achieve anything you put your mind to. If we all measured ourselves against our age, we would never accomplish anything in this lifetime. Let's look at Farah Gray, who began his entrepreneurial journey at the age of 6 selling home-made lotion and hand-painted rocks to his neighbours. By the age of 10 years old together with his group Urban Neighbourhood Enterprise Economic Club (UNEEC), they had managed to raise $15,000 to invest in various business ventures with some failing. However, within the first year, UNEEC had managed to grow its value to $100,000. This business later failed due to complications, however, that did not stop Farah as he continued investing. At the age of 14, he became the youngest African-American self-made millionaire after selling his Farah-Out Foods Company. To top it all off, he went on to become the most inexperienced advisor on the board of the Las Vegas Chamber of Commerce. In 2006 he was awarded an honorary doctorate, becoming the youngest African-American to be awarded this accolade from a black college or university. Today Farah is regarded as one of the greatest business minds to walk this earth.

Grow in maturity but maintain your inner child, the child that has dreams without restriction, the child that believes that they can be whatever they want to be. When it is all said and done let these be your words "I'm happy to report that my inner child is still ageless," James Broughton.

Remember that "Sometimes too late is just in time."

– C.J. CARLYON

ABOUT THE AUTHOR

Dave Smart is the Founder and CEO of Inspire Speaking, a public speaking company special-izing in education and empowerment. A Quantity Surveyor by profession, Dave has managed multi-million infrastructure and building projects. A true leader in this generation who aspires to spark passion, desire, and curiosity amongst the readers. Mr. Smart lives in Nottinghamshire in England. Visit his website: www.inspire-speaking.com

Printed in Great Britain
by Amazon